Between the Pieces

Paul White Ministries
P.O. Box 985
Poplar Bluff, MO 63902
USA

www.paulwhiteministries.org

Published in Collaboration with IONgdw | www.iongdw.com
Cover and Book Design by Jeffrey M. Hall | www.iongdw.com

Cover painting: Calvary, central panel of a triptych by Maerten van Heemskerck c.1547

ISBN: 978-0-9895419-0-9

For Worldwide Distribution, Printed in the U.S.A.

First Printing: 2013

Between the Pieces

What Really Happened at the Cross?

PAUL WHITE

Acknowledgments

I want to thank the wonderful people of Midland Church for their constant encouragement and endless inspiration. In particular, I am blessed to have such a wonderful group of godly men and women surrounding me on my church board and pastoral staff. Special thanks to Gary Hall, Delmar Manns, Russell Cross, Rick and Lovetia White, Michael White, Tony Kirkley, Bridget White and Trina Morey. You keep everything working on a day-to-day basis which affords me the time to write these things down. In my first book I called Midland Church "a pastor's dream." Apparently, I am still dreaming.

Contributions come in different ways and all of them make a profound difference on the finished product: Amanda Casey provided her excellent editorial skills to which I am abundantly grateful; my good friend Sloan Parker exchanged many emails and text messages with me offering inspiration and insight at several key points along the way; John Sheasby—a man of God like few others—was available to talk and share revelation on scripture during this process and his help was immense.

Nothing in my life would be the same without my lover and co-dreamer, the beautiful NaTasha. You are a wife and a mother, but you are also my friend.

Finally to my son Lukas and my daughter Lauren, you are always on my mind and in my heart. May I paint an image of fatherhood to you that always makes our Daddy look good.

Contents

Prologue

I once heard a divinity professor call *Hebrews*, "The least studied epistle in the American church." I'm not sure if his proclamation was based upon research or just a personal opinion formed through years of observation. Though he did not qualify it, I couldn't help but believe he might be right, for I am a product of the church, and I had only heard this great letter given in snippets and quotes.

The more I dug into the glorious "Letter to the Hebrews," the more confused I became as to why we knew so little about such a voluminous book. Full of rich comparisons and luscious illustrations of Christ's superiority, the only conclusions I have come to are both unsatisfactory. One, we think since its written to the Hebrews, it doesn't apply to us, and two, we are so covenant confused we simply can't see the distinction the author is so clearly making as to which covenant we are currently under, and why.

The book you are reading is not a dissertation on the Book of Hebrews. In fact, much of what you are going to read is pulled from many other sources, but the spirit of the *Letter to the Hebrews* should be felt throughout. The author (many argue it is Paul but I find it insignificant) is writing to a specific group of people (Hebrews/Jews) to prove to them the superiority of Christ to every other form of spiritualism and religion they have ever known (i.e., angels, Moses, Aaron, Levitical priesthood, tabernacle, etc.). When this foundation is laid, he then establishes the New Covenant as superior in every way to the one they had functioned beneath for so long – Mosaic Covenant – and had learned to define themselves by.

What we are going to try and accomplish in the coming pages is a well-defined distinction between covenants, so that the reader can have a clear picture of which one he is presently functioning under. To do this, we return to the cross of Christ, where the death of Jesus was forever changing the normalcy of religion into the supernatural experience of heavenly relationship.

My own, personal revelation of what Jesus accomplished at Calvary was a life-changing experience that led me deeper into the knowledge of the Father's love and His unending grace. As I began to understand what Jesus was actually doing on the cross and to comprehend what He was finishing when He declared "It is finished," I felt that the information was too powerful to keep to myself. I wanted everyone to know that Jesus was not only dying on a cross, but that His death was our death (2 Corinthians 5:14); His new life is our life (5:15); His finished work had reconciled the entire world back to God and that God no longer held man's sins against them (5:19). I clung to – and still do – the powerful concept that God took Jesus, who knew no sin, and made Him to be sin for us, so that we *might be made the righteousness of God in Him"* (2 Corinthians 5:21).

But somewhere along the way, while trying to reveal that God is no longer mad at mankind and that all sin was sufficiently punished in the body of His Son, something subtle and troubling began to occur. Without realizing what I was doing, I had begun to put the Father and the Son at odds. Calvary was becoming the scene of a great cosmic battle, not so much between God and Satan, but between God and His Son. I insinuated the Father killed His own Son, execution style, with the only concession being that Jesus was at least willing to be a participant in the event. I was fully aware that the cross did not sneak up on Jesus, and that He was indeed born to die. But while I understood that what He was doing was having my sins punished IN His body, I was beginning to present it in a way that had Him actually being punished Himself.

The revelations laid out in this book are not new, nor are they exclusive. This is simply the journey that I have been on in learning more of the fullness of Christ's Finished Work. It has cleaned up my image of the Father, and put in proper perspective what was happening at the cross. The curtain has been pulled back, and I have learned more of what was really going on when Jesus suffered and died. Misconceptions have been cleared up and pre-conceived notions have been found wanting.

On the other side of this revelation, I have found a new appreciation for the Finished Work. It has also allowed me to see the cross in a new light. Now I view Calvary as the turning point in man's direction and as the confirmation of God's love. It is the physical seal on a spiritual covenant, and the externalization of how God chooses to deal with humanity.

Together, we will go from how the early church initially felt about the death of Christ into a fuller, more complete revelation of where they ended up on the topic. As we see their development, we will understand what scriptures and events brought them to these conclusions, and how we too can arrive at a similar destination.

We will see Jesus pointing His audience to the appropriate prophecies of His death so they would understand the reasons for the cross. We will go with Apostle Paul as he changes the world and introduces it to Christianity, becoming both its founding father and its greatest ambassador.

Finally, we will sit ringside at the cutting of another covenant, one most Christians spend little time investigating, to learn why a simple passing between the pieces was the single most significant event in the history of the world, right on par with the Cross itself.

In totality, I hope this book accomplishes a better understanding of covenantal relationship. I will attempt to do this in two ways, both dealing with our title, *Between the Pieces*. On the surface, we will show you the moment when God walked between the pieces of animal sacrifice on that fateful night with Abraham, establishing a covenant of promise. Deeper, where there is "precept upon precept," we will go between the pieces of covenant, differentiating between them and digging out the nuggets of truth that are reserved for those willing to dive in and learn what happens between the lines.

I hope you enjoy the journey as much as I have enjoyed writing it down. It's not all-inclusive – no examination of covenant ever is. The honor of uncovering the glories of what God has finished on your behalf is all yours. When you finish this book I don't suspect you will have full revelation of covenantal goodness, but I hope you have a desire to learn more of what has been paid for on your behalf. A

Testament has been written and the testator has died. Now it is time to find out what is in your copy of the will.

Chapter 1

An Eyewitness Testimony

IT seems the whole world is well aware of an execution that took place on a small hill just outside the walls of Jerusalem nearly 2000 years ago. As famous as the events that happened on that hill called Calvary may be to us now, the brutal beating and horrific crucifixion of a young, Jewish carpenter named Jesus was neither important to, nor worth consideration by, the hand that had authorized such a killing. The mighty Roman Empire, with its newly perfected method of hanging criminals and strangers on vertical pieces of wood, hardly noticed when one of its underling administrators named Pontius Pilate carved the title "King of the Jews" and hung it over the head of one of the unfortunate ones. For them, it was an execution meant to maintain stability with a vocal religious minority in the backwaters of the Empire. For the rest of us, it was the single most important event in the long history of the world.

To those that believe that Jesus is the Son of God, this crucifixion was more than a Roman execution. For us, it is THE Crucifixion; the pivotal event that was "foreordained before the foundation of the world" (1 Peter 1:20). Calvary was a sacrifice; a burnt offering; the paying of the sin-ransom. What that carpenter named Jesus was accomplishing was the fulfillment of an old system and the ushering in of a new. The "last Adam" was accelerating us out of our old identity with the "first Adam" and into a whole new world of possibilities and better promises (Hebrews 8:6).

Much focus has been made over the centuries, through print, preaching and even film, on the physical aspects of Christ's death. I will refer to this as the *physicality* of the cross. This would include the actual beating, striping and mocking of Jesus, along with the crown of thorns, the hammering of the nails and the piercing of His side. We all have our own personal vision of this that has been shaped by Hollywood, and we know the painful emotions that are evoked when we see these scenes played out. Physically, the cross was brutal, as is obvious.

However, I don't wish to focus you, the reader, on the physicality of the cross. That's not to say it is not important, or that we won't refer to it at all, but I want our focus to be somewhere else. I want to take us behind the curtain, to see what was happening beyond where we can see. I will refer to this point of view as the *spirituality* of the cross.

Those standing near what the locals called "Golgatha," or "place of the skull," thought they were seeing just another afternoon of brutal murder. Even the disciples who had followed Jesus through His ministry were scattered and confused. Fortunately, the eye-witness accounts of that event were not written down for several decades, allowing those who were there to view the scene from the other side of the cross, divorced from the overwhelming feelings that such a moment could produce. If hindsight truly is 20/20, then the writers of both the Gospels and the Epistles had time to put the crucifixion of Jesus into the proper perspective, and to finally come to the revelation knowledge of what Jesus was actually accomplishing through His death.

Restoring the Marred Visage

My heart is to present God with as much love and compassion as I believe the Word says He has. I want to show forth Jesus in such a way that people respond, "I have never seen Jesus like that." I am under the persuasion that, if left alone to say simply what the Word declares Him saying and doing what the scriptures describe Him as doing, He is enough to transform both the natural world and your personal world.

How dare I, or anyone else, do anything to sully the picture of God that Jesus spent His earthly ministry trying to establish. When the disciples asked to see the Father, Jesus responded, "He that hath seen me hath seen the Father" (John 14:9), meaning that whatever you see Jesus do, you are seeing what the Father would do (conversely, whatever Jesus doesn't do, such as give someone leprosy or kill someone, don't expect the Father to do it!). When a Samaritan village rejected Jesus, certain disciples wanted to call down fire from heaven and consume the villagers, like the prophet Elijah had done. Jesus rebuked them, and declared, "You do not know what manner of spirit you are of. For the Son of Man did not come to destroy men's lives but to save them" (Luke 9:55, 56). He was on a constant mission to change man's perception of His Father.

When dealing with the Pharisees, the religious leaders of that day, Jesus once challenged them to read their own scriptures and to "…go and learn what this means: 'I desire mercy and not sacrifice.'" (Matthew 9:13). He was quoting from the book of Hosea, which they had easy access to. Apparently, they did not heed His advice, as a few chapters later He admonishes them for not doing as He said (Matthew 12:7). Even here, Jesus is attempting to change the religious perception the people had of His Father, and to show the world the love that He has.

Perhaps the problem in that day was similar to the one I fear we have now. Knowing Jesus only in the flesh, they had trouble identifying with Him in the Spirit. They couldn't conceptualize the things He was saying as being heavenly instead of earthly. A prime example of this is when, in John 4, He tells them He has meat to eat that they don't know about, and they wonder if someone has come along and fed Him. He then tries to move them from thinking in the natural to thinking in the spiritual by saying, "My food is to do the will of Him who sent Me, and to finish His work" (John 4:32-34).

If we stop our revelation of what Jesus did in the realm of the natural, then we will walk away from scenes of Calvary with ideas that sound like, "If Jesus did all of that for me, surely the least I could do is live for Him." With that mentality, we have dwelt on the physicality of the cross and felt a physical guilt and a rational loss. That veil keeps us from seeing anything deeper than a natural death, and we miss a powerful, spiritual, truth.

Apostle Paul warned the Corinthian church of this mentality when he reminded them that their position in Christ is not dependent on identifying with the physicality of Jesus but on the spirituality of His finished work:

"Therefore, from now on, we regard no one according to the flesh. Even though we have known Christ according to the flesh, yet now we know Him thus no longer." (2 Corinthians 5:16)

Paul is saying that even though many of his readers knew Jesus when He was on this earth, now their knowledge and faith in Him is not in what they saw and heard but in whom He was inside of them. Perhaps a more literal rendering can be found in the NIV translation, which takes the reader out of the realm of the natural:

"So from now on we regard no one from a worldly point of view. Though we once regarded Christ in this way, we do so no longer." (2 Corinthians 5:16 NIV)

With the concept of viewing the cross in spiritual terms, let's take a look at a verse that is often used to describe a physical scene, but keep in mind that a spiritual lesson is being taught here as well.

"Behold, My Servant shall deal prudently; He shall be exalted and extolled and be very high. Just as many were astonished at you, so His visage was marred more than any man, and His form more than the sons of men; so shall He sprinkle many nations. Kings shall shut their mouths at Him; for what had not been told them they shall see, and what they had not heard they shall consider." (Isaiah 52:13-15)

Through the lens of the physical, I see an obvious prophecy dealing with Jesus being so marred by beatings and pain on His way to the cross that His form was considered not human. But based on what I know Jesus came to do, which was make the Father appear merciful and loving, I think these verses are telling us that the "visage" (appearance) of God had been so marred that mankind did not recognize His true form.

By the time Jesus arrived, God had been given a bad name, and Jesus came to reveal a new name to them, which He claimed to have done in John 17:6, "I have manifested Your name to the men whom You have given me out of the world." "Abba," a name that Israel had never called God before, was heard in the streets every day, shouted by little children when calling their fathers. It means, "Daddy," and Jesus used it in the Garden of Gethsemane (Mark 14:36), revealing a new picture of the Father's love and affection.

This was an image that "had not been told them," and that before this, "they had not heard," (Isaiah 52:15) but now, due to a new image of the Father portrayed in Jesus, they would see it and be forced to consider it.

I hope to help you see it, and to consider such a relationship as well. Perhaps we can look past the sullied picture of the Father the church world has portrayed over the past several generations, and instead see how He was intended to look. Maybe we can move on from the physicality of the cross and into a place where the spiritual aspects of that great event become both relevant and necessary. I don't claim to reveal new revelations to you, for they are not new, simply overlooked and long forgotten. Under the surface of scriptures we have known and quoted are layers of truth that are rich and deep, full of nuggets of God's wisdom that have always revealed our inheritance and our rightful place.

Calvary was more than an execution of a man falsely accused; Calvary was the physical representation of a covenant that had been cut centuries before and was the ultimate in God's design for His creation. The crucifixion was not a crime scene where God killed His Son, for this paints God as murderous and at odds with His own creation. If God didn't require Abraham to kill his own son Isaac, why should we be left with the idea that God killed His own Son on a cross? The pristine image of His Father as portrayed to man was vitally important to Jesus, and should be equally vital to us who are ambassadors for Christ, and "able ministers of the New Testament" (2 Corinthians 3:6).

An Eyewitness Testimony

The best way to get a complete understanding of an event that we did not personally witness is to examine the testimony of someone who actually did. All four gospels record the death, burial and resurrection of our Lord Jesus, meaning it must have been a highlight moment in both His life and in the writers' examination of His life. These accounts give us a detailed look at the physicality of the cross, which shapes what we know and believe about Christ's death.

As good as these accounts are, one must go a little farther down the road of events in order to see what those witnesses actually *thought* about what they were seeing. I propose that when they were witnessing the events of the Passion and the day-to-day actions of Jesus, they understood very little. For instance, take Jesus' triumphal entry into Jerusalem:

> *"His disciples did not understand these things at first; but when Jesus was glorified, then they remembered that these things were written about Him and that they had done these things to Him."* (John 12:16)

Another example would be found in Luke, when Jesus explains (for the third time) that He is going to Jerusalem to fulfill prophecy. He even names His killers!

> *"For He will be delivered to the Gentiles and will be mocked and insulted and spit upon. They will scourge Him and kill Him. And the third day He will rise again."* (Luke 18:32, 33)

That seems pretty plain doesn't it? Yet, the disciples missed it.

> *"But they understood none of these things; this saying was hidden from them, and they did not know the things which were spoken."* (Luke 18:34)

I believe the point the Spirit is making through the text is that it was going to take hindsight given by God in order to see what Jesus was truly accomplishing at the cross. While man would witness it, he wouldn't comprehend it until after the resurrection. Jesus identifies the Gentiles as the guilty party, which would have been obvious from the outset; however, there are even deeper truths to be learned, and the Spirit is about to unveil them.

Let's take the eyewitness account of Peter, a man who was at least in the proximity of the cross on the day that Jesus died. He had spent some time the night before in the courtyard outside the hall of Pontius Pilate and, as we all know, he had ultimately denied that he even knew Jesus. We pick up his account in Acts 3, when he approaches the steps of the temple in Jerusalem, accompanied by another eyewitness to the crucifixion, the Apostle John.

Peter and John go to the temple at the ninth hour of the day, which in Jewish terms was 3 p.m. This is an important time of day, which we will bring relevance to in later chapters, but for now, just note that they were entering through the gate called "Beautiful," as they had no doubt done many times before, perhaps even with Jesus during His ministry. A lame man sits at the temple gate asking alms of those who enter, including Peter and John. Peter fixes his eyes on those of the lame man and says, "Silver and gold I do not have, but what I do have I give you: In the name of Jesus Christ of Nazareth, rise up and walk." (Acts 3:6) Though we are sure the disciples have used the name of Jesus to do great things before (Luke 10:17), this is the first time it has been vocalized in the New Testament, making this healing a remarkable account.

Peter has already begun his amazing journey into the revelation of God's glory. He was filled with the Spirit on the Day of Pentecost in Acts 2, and accelerated from denial of Christ to proclamation of His glorious name (Acts 2:38). This healing is a further example of him walking deeper into what he is learning about God.

Now, let's pick up the story after the man leaps up and walks into the temple, prompting the crowd to lose itself in wild excitement.

> "So when Peter saw it, he responded to the people: 'Men of Israel, why do you marvel at this? Or why look so intently on us, as though by our own power or godliness we had made this man walk?'" (Acts 3:12)

Peter is doing something almost foreign to the modern church: deflecting attention away from himself and what he has done to deserve this power to heal. So many times, we hear that if we read more, fast more, give more and do more, we will be more anointed and used of God. Little do many people realize they are being prompted to earn from God what is supposed to be freely given by His grace!

> "The God of Abraham, Isaac, and Jacob, the God of our fathers, glorified His Servant Jesus, whom you delivered up and denied in the presence of Pilate, when he was determined to let Him go." (Acts 3:13)

With the opening line in his sermon, Peter gives us our first hint into his perception of Calvary. He indicates who he believes is responsible for delivering Jesus to Pontius Pilate, and he further indicates that he knew Pilate was determined to let Christ go. This determination on the part of Pilate must have been so evident that even from Peter's vantage point in the court yard he knew there was little chance of a conviction.

> *"But you denied the Holy One and the Just, and asked for a murderer to be granted to you."* (Acts 3:14)

It is obvious that Peter is accusing the Jews in his audience of desiring Barabbas, a convicted murderer, to be released to them in place of the innocent Jesus. He calls Jesus "the Holy One," putting Him on equal footing with the Father, and "Just," indicating that Jesus' judgments are righteous. But did you catch what else Peter does? Look at the accusation contained in the first three words of the verse. Now, access all of those old Sunday school lessons on which you were raised about a certain disciple warming his hands by the fire while Jesus stands trial, and then the crowing of the rooster that marks his failure in denying his Master.

It's Peter who is the chief of denial! It's Peter who could be reminded of his proclamation to Jesus that if all others left Him, he wouldn't (Matthew 26:33). Yet, it's that same Peter who makes no mention of his own denial in this sermon.

In my opinion, this is one of the most under-preached, beautiful scriptures concerning the power of the New Covenant. Once you realize that the old man is gone and your new man is created "in righteousness and true holiness," (Ephesians 4:24) you stop living in the guilt of the past. You stop worrying about being the one that denied Him and you start standing in the provisions of the New Covenant of grace and peace. Peter is the one who denied Jesus, yet he stands in the temple that day as if he never had. What an example! May you walk through this world as if you have never failed.

Because Peter stood with the power of the Holy Ghost in the knowledge of forgiveness and preached this message, not one person cried, "Wait a minute, *we* denied Him? *You're* the one that denied Him!" Grace is your forgiveness, and your boldness.

When Does the Rooster Crow?

I want to take an aside for just a moment, for this bit of information regarding Peter's accusation of denial without a hint of his own past guilt is just too good to pass up. Jesus' prophecy to Peter that he would deny Him actually entails an important fact about the spirituality of the cross.

> *"Then Jesus said to them, 'All of you will be made to stumble because of Me this night, for it is written: 'I will strike the Shepherd, and the sheep of the flock will be scattered.' But after I have been raised, I will go before you to Galilee.' Peter answered and said to Him, 'Even if all are made to stumble because of You, I will never be made to stumble.' Jesus said to him, 'Assuredly, I say to you that this night, before the rooster crows, you will deny Me three times.' Peter said to Him, 'Even if I have to die with You, I will not deny You!' And so said all the disciples."* (Matthew 26:31-35)

To be fair to Peter, Jesus opened the speech by declaring "All of you will be made to stumble because of Me this night," and then the passage closes with all the disciples saying the same thing as Peter. This means that Peter wasn't the only one who said he would be faithful and then didn't keep his word, yet the story follows no one into his denial as specifically as it does Peter. Perhaps this is done to take us to the powerful sermon of Acts 3, to show us the power of redemption to not only remove our sin, but to remove our consciousness of that sin.

Jesus is quoting from Zechariah 13:7, effectively calling Himself "the Shepherd," and His disciples "the sheep of the flock." He is going far beyond hinting as to what His death is all about, by quoting a verse that puts the sword of God's judgment into a shepherd, who is obviously dying for the protection of the sheep. This speaks volumes concerning what Jesus told them earlier:

> *"I am the good shepherd. The good shepherd gives His life for the sheep."* (John 10:11)

Peter hears this proclamation and has difficulty seeing Jesus' death as anything more than a loss and a murder, while Jesus is trying to take them beyond the physical and into the spiritual. In this hour of physical danger, Jesus is revealing a spiritual truth about the New Covenant; not only does He give the reason for His death, but He proclaims a great truth about that death. The truth is found in His illustration of the rooster and its action.

What does a rooster do? He crows. Let's not make it too complex; simple is often better. Does the rooster crow all of the time? Actually, yes; there is no specific time of day that a rooster will crow (the idea that it only sits on a fence post and crows at sunrise is more fiction than fact). However, the trial of Jesus takes place in the middle of the night, and the accusations against Him will be complete before the sun comes up. Within context of Jesus' trial, the crowing of a rooster would declare the dawn of a new day, and I believe that is exactly the point Jesus is making to Peter. "The rooster will sound an alarm Peter, but just remember, his alarm means the sun is coming up."

In the New Covenant of God's grace and mercy, the sun is always coming up on your life. There is no need to rehash the events of yesterday, or to mourn the faults you piled up in your old creation, for it isn't midnight in your soul any longer. The night of fear and condemnation is past and you are a new creation. The rooster is crowing to declare that your denials and your sins are gone. Hear the crowing today; God is reminding you that it's a new day in your world of possibilities!

"You killed the Prince of life"

By Acts 3, Peter has learned his lesson, and the guilt associated with the denial is apparently gone from his consciousness. Armed with the insight that only hindsight provides, Peter now moves the responsibility of the crucifixion beyond only the Romans (Gentiles) and onto his present audience.

> "And killed the Prince of life, whom God raised from the dead, of which we are witnesses." (Acts 3:15)

Peter reveals three things of which he is currently sure: the Jewish audience before him killed the Prince of life; Jesus is the Prince of life; Peter was a witness to the resurrection, which he attributed to the power of God. Peter is stating that these three things are the basis of his sermon, and if you read the remainder of it, it doesn't go much deeper than that theologically.

We can see Peter's progressive revelation of the finished work if we look at his life through the book of Acts, but we can get better insight into what that finished work come to represent to him by reading his letter.

> *"For to this you were called, because Christ also suffered for us, leaving us an example, that you should follow His steps:"* (1 Peter 2:21)

Somewhere along the way, between Acts 3, where his version of Calvary was "you killed the Prince of life," Peter has now concluded, "Christ suffered for us." His revelation of the cross now includes the knowledge that Calvary was Christ suffering as our substitute. This is progressively moving Peter from the physicality of the cross to the spirituality of the cross.

> *"Who committed no sin, nor was deceit found in His mouth."* (1 Peter 2:22)

Here, Peter declares that Jesus was sinless, which is a proclamation which declares His death to be unjust in natural terms, since only a guilty man was supposed to die. I don't believe that Peter ever doubted this point of theology, but at this time he decides to write it down. By the way, this verse answers to the point made at the end of the previous verse, "…that you should follow His steps." Following His steps is not a demand for us to suffer as Christ did, but for us to commit no sin and not have deceit spew forth from our mouth. In His death, Christ is our redemption; in His lifestyle, Christ is our example.

> *"Who, when He was reviled, did not revile in return; when He suffered, He did not threaten, but committed Himself to Him who judges righteously."* (1 Peter 2:23)

Peter is starting to lean toward a prophetic passage of the cross with this verse, a connection we will explore in great detail in the next chapter. For now, let's point out that Peter recognized the silence of Jesus on the cross, and His lack of retaliatory response as noble, not a sign of weakness or guilt. He also sees Calvary as a judgment on the part of God, though we have little evidence as to what was being judged. But don't stop here, for Peter's culmination of revelation is coming up.

> *"Who Himself bore our sins in His own body on the tree, that we, having died to sins, might live for righteousness — by whose stripes you were healed."* (1 Peter 2:24)

There it was! Did you catch it? Peter has figured it out; moving past Calvary as an assassination, he now concludes "Why" Jesus died. With no sin of His own, He doesn't qualify for judgment, since there is nothing to be judged. Thus, Peter is concluding that Jesus was bearing our sins INSIDE His body on that tree, so that all of us could have our death in His death. This allows us to live for righteousness' sake.

Paul said it another way to the Romans, but with the same intent:

> *"And having been set free from sin, you became slaves of righteousness."* (Romans 6:18)

Christ's death was a judgment against sin, this is for sure. His death set us free from the slave camp of sin and made us a new kind of slave. We are not slaves to God, but rather we are His Sons (Galatians 4:7); instead, we are slaves to righteousness. In other words, because Jesus bore our sins in His body at Calvary, and God judged them righteously, I can't help but be righteous!

Chapter 2

Connect the Dots

"*Who Himself bore our sins in His own body on the tree, that we, having died to sins, might live for righteousness – by whose stripes you were healed.*" (1 Peter 2:24)

We tend to think that the early church fathers had a firm grasp on every theological point from the moment they first began to spread the good news, but even a precursory look at the book of Acts will prove otherwise. As these men progressed deeper into their lives and ministries, they began to learn more of the grace of God and how His grace was a permanent replacement for their Jewish ideologies and norms. The cross would begin to take pre-eminence as the focal point, and more importantly, served as the turning point in God's plan for humanity. As these apostles developed a more complete concept of Calvary, they began to filter everything they had ever known, read, or understood, through this event. In like manner, Peter's concept of the cross developed over a period of time.

By the time he wrote his epistles, Peter determined that Calvary was best summed up as the place where sin was judged in the body of a sacrifice and that it was the pre-cursor to a resurrection of life. In other words, what started in his mind as an execution changed to a substitution; with Christ as the bearer of our sins, dying a necessary death for us, to provide us with new life.

As we will see in later chapters, the disciples of Jesus and the apostles of the early church had a rather deep understanding of the scriptures that make up our Old Testament, which would have constituted most of the inspired writings of their day. When Paul states that "all Scripture is given by inspiration of God, and is profitable for doctrine, for reproof, for correction, for instruction in righteousness," (2Timothy 3:16) he is actually referring to the only scripture that Timothy has: those from his childhood (3:17), the Old Testament.

Paul made a practice of using these scriptures to explain and testify about the kingdom of God, "persuading them concerning Jesus from both the Law of Moses and the Prophets, from morning till evening" (Acts 28:23). When Paul taught from the law and the prophets, he did not use the law to browbeat or to even instruct, rather it was to show how Jesus had fulfilled the law and lived it to perfection. When he spoke from the prophets, he did not do it to put the arrival of Messiah out beyond his audience, but to show Jesus as the Messiah, and to paint Him as the ultimate fulfillment of prophecy.

This process of "connecting the dots" was a tried and true method of taking point A from the Torah (Old Testament) and letting it lead to point B in the life and death of Christ. Those old, familiar verses that these men had known since childhood were now jumping off the page with brand new meaning. What had once been mere stories of Israel coming out of Egypt, eating manna, and crossing over the Jordan River were now metaphors for coming out of the slave camp of sin, eating the broken body of the Lord Jesus, and coming through the rivers of the Spirit into a whole new world of rest.

It was Jesus who had taught them to use the Old Testament in this manner. In a conversation with the Jewish ruler, Nicodemus, Jesus pointed to the brazen serpent lifted on a pole by Moses, to alleviate the viper bite sustained by many Israelites. "And as Moses lifted up the serpent in the wilderness, even so must the Son of Man be lifted up, that whoever believes in Him should not perish but have eternal life" (John 3:14, 15). He did it again on the day of His resurrection when He encountered two disciples on the road from Jerusalem to Emmaus. Supernaturally blinded so they would not recognize Him, these disciples revealed that they thought Jesus was the one who would redeem Israel. But after His death, and with His tomb now empty, they weren't sure what to believe. Jesus then begins, "...at Moses and all the Prophets, He expounded to them in all the Scriptures the things concerning Himself" (Luke 24:27). So it is Christ Himself that introduces this method of connecting the dots to find the answers.

I think this is what Peter is doing for his reader when he takes us from the spirituality of the cross ("bore sins in His body," "died to sins," "live for righteousness") back to the physicality ("by whose stripes…") and then right back to the spiritual ("…you were healed"). To make this jump, he has to be leaping from one dot to the next, and with an understanding of the Old Testament, these leaps are not hard to discern.

"On the tree"

The first indication in 1 Peter 2:24 that Peter is making a connection between the Old Testament and the happenings of the cross are found in his specific wording of where Jesus died. He states that Jesus bore our sins in His own body, "on the tree," which points his audience to the specific act of dying on the cross. But I believe that Peter is taking his more astute readers into deeper waters.

Those who were familiar with the writings of Moses would be well aware of the importance of someone dying on a tree. Moses spoke of this type of execution in his fifth book:

> "If a man has committed a sin deserving of death, and he is put to death, and you hang him on a tree, his body shall not remain overnight on the tree, but you shall surely bury him that day, so that you do not defile the land which the LORD your God is giving you as an inheritance; for he who is hanged is accursed of God." (Deuteronomy 21:22, 23)

The Jewish leaders who were responsible for the death of Jesus were well aware of this passage, and knew that it would lend credibility to their argument that Jesus was a blasphemer. If He died on a cross, He would fall beneath the curse of this Old Testament passage, and those standing at Calvary would be forced to admit that they were witnessing someone who had "committed a sin worthy of death" and that God had cursed Him.

Notice that the Pharisees were quick to put Jesus on a cross to fulfill the part of this verse that served their purpose, but they were also equally quick to make sure that He was off the cross before the sun went down so they would not incur the wrath of God for leaving the body "all night upon the tree." I find it a curious point of religion that while one part of a verse gets full attention, the other often goes unnoticed. Jesus was certainly not guilty of committing any sin, much less "a sin worthy of death," but no one worried too much about that in their mad dash to make sure their land was not defiled by failing to "bury him that day."

I will deal with this passage in more detail in the next chapter, including an in depth look at how the Apostle Paul interpreted it in light of the New Covenant of grace. It is a vital examination of the graduation from Old Covenant to New, and we will give it the treatment it deserves. For now, let us go with Peter on his journey back into the Old Testament to connect the dots between what he saw at Calvary and what he believed had actually happened.

"By whose stripes..."

"...and by His stripes we are healed." Peter pulls this line directly from Isaiah 53:5, changing only one word to reflect that this is in the reader's past, not his future ("by whose stripes you were healed"). The reference shows us that Peter believed the 53rd chapter of Isaiah was speaking of Christ's crucifixion, and that the stripes He bore there were part of a finished work; so finished, in fact, that its effects were irreversible and eternal.

To us, on the other side of the cross, the 53rd chapter is obviously dealing with the death of Jesus. However, to someone living in the time of Christ, this chapter is a relatively non-specific one in regards to exactly how the victim dies or even who the victim might be. Whoever it is, is "cut off from the land of the living," and is dying "for the transgressions of My people" (Isaiah 53:8). There is no direct reference to the victim dying on a cross, or to piercings by thorns or nails. We read that he is "wounded," "bruised," and "striped," but we can't be sure it was happening at Calvary.

This makes Peter's connection so remarkable. He is tying the events he witnessed outside the walls of Jerusalem, when Jesus hung and died, to the prophecy of one who would "carry our sorrows," and be "wounded for our transgressions." One reference to one verse within one chapter would fill the gaps of hundreds of years, effectively placing Jesus in the center of that great chapter, bringing meaning and clarity to what had been only a hope and a dream before.

If Peter saw Jesus within the text of this great chapter, and the Holy Spirit deemed it worthy of inclusion in the canon of scripture, then we are seeing divine sanction on the interpretation of this passage. This allows us to glean tremendous truths from the verses of Isaiah 53 and to learn remarkable details about the death of Jesus. Let us look at a few of the passages to learn a bit more about how the world into which Christ came would view His death. Remember, Peter pointed out the dots, now we must connect them.

> "Who has believed our report? And to whom has the arm of the LORD been revealed?" (Isaiah 53:1)

You may recall the verses from Isaiah 52 that we used in our last chapter, to show how the world might have had an improper view of God by the time Jesus arrived. This is the reason the 53rd chapter opens the way it does. John picks up on this verse in his gospel:

> "But although He had done so many signs before them, they did not believe in Him, that the word of Isaiah the prophet might be fulfilled, which he spoke: 'Lord, who has believed our report? And to whom has the arm of the LORD been revealed?'" (John 12:37-38)

Notice that John adds the word 'Lord' to the front of the passage, taking the liberty to show that the text is written from the perspective of Isaiah. This sets the tone for the chapter, as now the author will be showing you an audience's perspective of an execution, letting you see what they see and make interpretations at the same pace that they do. This becomes vital in understanding the mindset of the Jewish people at the time of Christ's death.

In his letter to the Romans, Paul uses this passage as well, to explain why Israel was experiencing wholesale rejection of Jesus, when he writes, "But they have not all obeyed the gospel. For Isaiah says, 'LORD, who has believed our report?'" (Romans 10:16)

"For He shall grow up before Him as a tender plant, and as a root out of dry ground." (Isaiah 53:2a)

Jesus is the "arm of the LORD" from Verse 1 and the capitalization of the pronouns "He" and "Him" show us that Jesus was prophesied to be that arm and to grow up in the sight of God. There can be no doubt that Isaiah, coupled with John and Paul seeing Jesus in this passage, and later Peter doing the same, is speaking about the first advent of Christ.

The most direct connection for this verse is found earlier in Isaiah's book, to show the lineage of Israel's future king:

"There shall come forth a Rod from the stem of Jesse, and a Branch shall grow out of his roots." (Isaiah 11:1)

The word "Rod" is better translated as "shoot" in Hebrew, meaning the natural lineage of Jesus would be an offshoot from the "stem" or "stump" of Jesse, who was the father of David. That which was cut off (the kingly lineage of Jesus through his forefather Jesse) will spring forth again (Jesus as "King of kings"). This prophecy declares the Messiah to be of kingly heritage, which we know Jesus to be.

A root growing out of dry ground is a tree defying the odds. Dry ground would define the world upon Jesus' arrival, and the fact that He survives and thrives is a testament to His divine lineage. It is the Father that guards and protects Him as a tender plant, despite the reasons He should fail. Jesus is not only the personification of grace, but it is grace that contributes to His survival. Think about how the deck is stacked against Him, so to speak. He is heralded as a king while only an infant, incapable of protecting Himself against those who would do Him harm. He garners no earthly wealth or possessions by which to finance His efforts. He acquires no formal education to give Him entrance into the synagogues and temples of which His ministry is so vital. He is born into a relatively crippled nation, in the forgotten part of a world power, with no prospect of ever escaping. It will take the protection of His Father to fulfill such a task of taking away the sin of the world in the face of such overwhelming odds.

"He has no form or comeliness; and when we see Him, there is no beauty that we should desire Him." (Isaiah 53:2b)

The Hebrew words used here for "form" and "comeliness" speak of a stately splendor. The Jerusalem Bible translates it, "Without beauty, without majesty (we saw him), no looks to attract our eyes." I won't bother to read into whether or not Jesus was handsome or homely (I have read works touting both points of view), for I don't feel this was the prophet's intent. I am personally under the persuasion that this text is showing that the disciples felt Jesus' appeal was in His words and His deeds, not in the natural things that are normally remembered of a man, such as his looks and personality. I'm not prepared to say they had forgotten what He looked like, but I think the argument could be made that they put little emphasis on what they remembered of Him physically, since there isn't a single description of His appearance in either the Gospels or the Epistles. The closest we get is John telling his Gnostic audience (the Gnostic's didn't believe that Christ had actually come in the flesh) in 1 John 1:1 that in regards to a physical Jesus, "we have seen with our eyes, which we have looked upon, and our hands have handled, concerning the Word of life."

The Apostle Paul added, "Therefore, from now on, we regard no one according to the flesh. Even though we have known Christ according to the flesh, yet now we know Him thus no longer" (2 Corinthians 5:16). As we discussed in our opening chapter, the meaning of this verse is obvious, however it could also contribute to the argument that the apostolic fathers recalled little of Jesus in physical terms, confining their memories and writings to the spiritual.

"He is despised and rejected by men, a man of sorrows and acquainted with grief. And we hid, as it were, our faces from Him; He was despised, and we did not esteem Him." (Isaiah 53:3)

Note that Jesus (we know it is Jesus because we have connected the dots) is not despised and rejected by God, but rather, "by men." In being despised, "we did not esteem Him." This word "esteem" is from the Hebrew word "chashab," meaning, "to think, to count, to regard, to reckon." So the prophet is saying that Jesus would be rejected by men and despised by them and they wouldn't regard him for who He was. In other words, at His death, man would want nothing to do with Him.

Please remember that this text is written hundreds of years before Jesus goes to the cross, and Isaiah is writing to a group of people about the death of someone, without getting specific as to exactly who it was. There is nothing in this passage that would lead someone in AD 33, standing at the foot of the cross, to read Isaiah 53 and say, "The man in this passage must be Jesus." It is simply a general prophecy about the death of the Messiah, but it never mentions, "Jesus of Nazareth."

However, prophecy doesn't have to be name specific. In this case, the information that is necessary for identifying who is dying is found in the *audience* that He is dying in front of. Someday, five hundred years or so after this is written, a group of people will see a man, and there will be no beauty in him that they should desire him. They will despise and reject this man that is acquainted with much sorrow. They will hide their faces from him and choose not to regard him for who he says he is. Based on this, we know the prophecy is identifying the audience at Calvary, and the wording is about to reflect their specific attitude towards that event.

> *"Surely He has borne our griefs and carried our sorrows; yet we esteemed Him stricken, smitten by God, and afflicted."* (Isaiah 53:4)

The crowd that witnessed Jesus' crucifixion is now speaking to us from the pages of Isaiah. They didn't realize who He was, but their immediate perception of the events at Calvary was that this man that was dying before them was "smitten of God." Remember, their knowledge of Mosaic law concerning the death of a man on a tree would have been enough for them to consider the crucifixion of Jesus as God smiting a man who had blasphemed by calling himself God.

Just because the crowd thought Jesus was smitten of God, does not mean that He was, and it doesn't mean that Isaiah thought the same. Notice the next verse, paying specific attention to the very first word.

> *"But He was wounded for our transgressions, He was bruised for our iniquities; the chastisement for our peace was upon Him, and by His stripes we are healed."* (Isaiah 53:5)

The word "but," is a conjunction, connecting the thought of the previous verse with the description of verse 5. It is the root of "rebuttal," so if you see "but," you are seeing something being refuted. In this case, the conjunction is not just a connection, it is actually coming against what the crowd originally thought. Read them back-to-back.

> *"We esteemed Him stricken, smitten by God, and afflicted. But He was wounded…"* (Isaiah 53:4, 5)

The crowd originally thought God was angry at the victim on the cross and that He was killing Him for blasphemy. But the prophet Isaiah shows that the same crowd will soon learn that He was actually being wounded for their transgressions and bruised for their iniquities. It was the chastisement of that group's discipline that was on Jesus, and their healing came through His stripes. He wasn't being forsaken by His Father; God wasn't ticked off at Jesus!

Jesus loved His group of disciples so passionately that He gave them a forewarning regarding the events at Calvary. He meant to assure them that His life was a glorification of God and that His death would be the same. He spoke of His pending death as the purpose for which, "I came to this hour" (John 12:27). In Verse 28, Jesus says aloud, "Father glorify Your name," and a voice came from heaven saying, "I have both glorified it and will glorify it again." Jesus turns to His disciples and says, "This voice did not come because of Me, but for your sake." This encounter with God was meant to set the disciples at ease in the face of impending crucifixion. Jesus was not going to the cross because God was angry at Him, and this incident was meant to prove as much.

Let's personalize it. At Calvary, Jesus was wounded for *my* transgressions, bruised for *my* iniquities, and by His stripes *I* am healed. He was chastised, or "disciplined" for our peace, meaning that *our sins* were disciplined in Jesus so that we can be at peace. These sins have been brought under subjection; our sins know who is boss! Why? Because of grace, sin shall no longer dominate you, for you are not under the law; you are under grace (Romans 6:14). It can't dominate; it has been disciplined.

"But He was wounded…"

In Acts 3:15, Peter accused the Jews in Jerusalem of killing Jesus, and we can concur that it was their insistence that put Him on a cross. But they certainly were not alone. The Romans had a hand in His death, with Pontius Pilate authorizing it, and the Roman soldiers carrying out the deed. With all the parties involved, it is impossible to lay the blame on only one person or one group of people.

"But He was wounded for our transgressions," tells us that there was a higher purpose for the death of Christ, and we can be certain that neither the Jews nor the Romans thought for a moment that *they* were punishing the sins of humanity in the body of Jesus. In fact, neither group would have the power to do so! This phrase, more than any other in the chapter, turns the spotlight onto God, taking the death of Jesus out of the hands of mortal men and placing into the very capable hands of the Father. If Jesus was truly wounded for our transgressions, then only God could place the transgressions there and judge them properly. This phrase demands the cross be viewed for its spirituality over its physicality.

What, if anything, was God doing behind the scenes? He was actually putting our sins into Jesus so that Jesus could die as a sacrifice, laying His life down willingly. God wasn't angry with Jesus at the cross, no more than He would kill His own Son; but God was angry with the sins of wicked humanity, and He had been every day (Psalm 7:11). In Christ, He found Himself a lamb (Genesis 22:8), and whenever the world killed Jesus, God was viewing our transgressions in Jesus, making His discipline, our discipline.

"By His stripes..."

This 5th verse is the one Peter is incorporating into his argument in 1 Peter 2:24, "by whose stripes you were healed." He changes the tense, putting our healing in the past rather than in our future, declaring the finished work of the cross to be finished entirely. Just as our sins have been sufficiently punished, so our sicknesses and our diseases have been paid for in Christ.

I have heard it argued that Isaiah 53:5 is pointing back to the opening verses of the same book, answering to a problem pointed out by the prophet.

> *"Why should you be stricken again? You will revolt more and more.*
> *The whole head is sick, and the whole heart faints."* (Isaiah 1:5)

Some teach that when Isaiah prophesies that by His stripes we will be healed, he wasn't referring to physical healing, but rather to this verse which describes Israel's head as sick and its heart as faint, and that Jesus would be stricken so that His stripes would be for their spiritual healing. This is often touted by those who deny that Jesus paid for our actual physical healing at the cross. They make a compelling argument, I'm sure. But to do so, they must ignore what those who walked with Jesus thought of the same passages regarding healing.

In Matthew's gospel, he takes the 53rd chapter of Isaiah, and due to the miracles he sees Jesus doing in His earthly ministry, he puts a little twist on it.

> *"When evening had come, they brought to Him many who were demon-possessed. And He cast out the spirits with a word, and healed all who were sick, that it might be fulfilled which was spoken by Isaiah the prophet, saying: 'He Himself took our infirmities and bore our sicknesses.'"* (Matthew 8:16, 17)

Matthew took Isaiah 53:4, where Jesus took our "griefs" and carried our "sorrows" and he rendered them closer to their Hebrew meanings, changing them to "infirmities" and "sicknesses." Either Matthew was confused as to what Jesus came to do, or he believed in one who could really take away sickness!

Man Did the Killing, God Did the Bruising

"Yet it pleased the LORD to bruise Him; He has put Him to grief."
(Isaiah 53:10)

Let me be very clear: I do not believe the Father killed His own Son at Calvary, but I do believe He saw all of our sins and our sicknesses in His Son and then bruised Him, effectively crushing the head of the serpent and taking the sting out of death. This puts the onus of responsibility for the cross from a physical standpoint on the hands of man, specifically, the Jewish leaders that demanded His death. However, this makes the cross a turning point in the realm of the Spirit. If God has been "pleased" then God is appeased, which all of the sacrifices of the Old Testament could never do. What was He bruising in Jesus?

He was bruising our sin, thus if God was pleased in doing so, why would He ever cease from being pleased now?

The writer to the Hebrews said it this way:

> *"Therefore, when He came into the world, He said: 'Sacrifice and offering You did not desire, but a body You have prepared for Me. In burnt offerings and sacrifices for sin You had no pleasure. Then I said, 'Behold, I have come – in the volume of the book it is written of Me – to do Your will, O God.'"* (Hebrews 10:5-7)

When Jesus "came into the world," He understood that the system of sacrificial offerings was not what the Father desired, thus He had prepared a body for Jesus. The Father derived no pleasure (He was never 'pleased') from the old Mosaic economy of redemption. So Jesus stated that "the volume of the book is written of Me," telling us that the whole of the Old Testament was speaking about His arrival. He further stated that He came, "to do Your will, O God."

> *"By that will we have been sanctified through the offering of the body of Jesus Christ once for all."* (Hebrews 10:10)

"That will" was the will of the Father that Jesus came to fulfill, and in allowing the body prepared for Him to be the carrier of the sins of the world, Jesus became that which appeased the Father: a truly worthy sacrifice for sin. God was pleased because, in punishing sins in Jesus, He didn't have to punish sins in the body of the sinner. Calvary was about the will of the Father being done through the offering of the body of Jesus Christ, "once for all." In short, Calvary was about us!

"Once for all"

Under the Old Covenant, every time a man sinned he was required to offer a sacrifice. Though they sacrificed bulls, goats, sheep and turtledoves, none of these could please the wrath of God. Then Jesus bore our sins in His body on the tree, and God viewed that satisfactory sacrifice as sufficient, "once for all." This leaves no stone unturned, or no sin unforgiven! There never needs to be another sacrifice for sin, as the "once for all" sacrifice covers every man, for all time. Due to this fact, "He adds, 'Their sins and their lawless deeds I will remember no more'" (Hebrews 10:17).

I hope you can see that God has been pleased through the death of Jesus, leaving nothing for you to do to please God. In our old church paradigm, we asked questions like, "Is your life pleasing to God?" and all of us would hang our heads, condemned in the knowledge that we were less than pleasing. When the pastor would point his finger at us and say, "Have you done everything you can this week for the Lord and the kingdom?" we knew we hadn't and we left the building determined to do better, but powerless to know how. May God raise up more voices that proclaim an appeased God, with no fear that such a message will produce people who are anything less than excellent. May we sing, teach, testify and preach of the finished work of the cross as if it is truly finished. When we are confronted with all the negative aspects of people's lives and their propensity to sin, may we be as the Apostle Paul, so convinced that what Jesus paid for at the cross is our answer, that we are determined to shut our mouths from proclaiming anything less.

> *"And I, brethren, when I came to you, did not come with excellence of speech or of wisdom declaring to you the testimony of God. For I determined not to know anything among you except Jesus Christ and Him crucified."* (1 Corinthians 2:1, 2)

Chapter 3

Christ Was Made a Curse

N ow that we have linked the Apostolic writings of the finished work to the Old Testament prophecies of the same, let's look a bit deeper into one of the key issues of Calvary. We mentioned the fact that Christ was made a curse in our previous chapter, but more dedication should be given to finding out precisely what that means.

Peter wrote that Jesus "bore our sins in His own body on the tree," and Moses wrote that he who was hanged on a tree "is accursed of God." This caused the crowd at Calvary to conclude that Jesus was "smitten of God." However, as we have established, it was actually the Jewish leaders, the Roman soldiers and various other players who put Jesus on the cross. But what do we do with that verse from Moses' writings? Could God simply ignore the mandate to curse the one hung on a tree?

> *"If a man has committed a sin deserving of death, and he is put to death, and you hang him on a tree, his body shall not remain overnight on the tree, but you shall surely bury him that day, so that you do not defile the land which the LORD your God is giving you as an inheritance; for he who is hanged is accursed of God."* (Deuteronomy 21:22, 23)

Various religions have been known to use this passage to speak disparagingly of the Christian philosophy that Christ's was a sacrificial death. They mock Christians for proclaiming Christ to be the redeemer of mankind through the cross, citing this Old Testament scripture as proof that Jesus was cursed by God, and thus disqualified as being the savior of the world. How can one be considered sinless that dies as a cursed man?

I cannot say, with any authority, what the early church felt about this passage immediately following Jesus' crucifixion. I would imagine, considering the vehement hatred spewed forth from the Pharisees towards Jesus during His time on earth, the propaganda surrounding His death was immense. It makes sense to envision the Jewish leaders reminding people in the weeks following His death that this passage from Deuteronomy could not be ignored. I would also presume that they used the argument to try and squelch any excitement regarding His resurrection.

While we may not know what the early church thought of Deuteronomy 21:22-23, we do know what the Apostle Paul thought of it, following his own personal revelation of the New Covenant. In his letter to the church at Galatia, Paul quotes Moses directly, unafraid to back down from such a damning verse, and actually uses it to transition the reader from a religion of works into a life of faith.

> *"Christ has redeemed us from the curse of the law, having become a curse for us (for it is written, 'Cursed is everyone who hangs on a tree'), that the blessing of Abraham might come upon the Gentiles in Christ Jesus, that we might receive the promise of the Spirit through faith."* (Galatians 3:13, 14)

Paul declares us free from the curse attached to the law due to the fact that Jesus became a curse for us. He establishes the argument on the same verses used by many to promote the opposite view. Using Deuteronomy 21:22-23, Paul does not deny that Jesus must naturally be considered cursed, but he sees the curse as a substitution rather than a punishment. In other words, Paul saw Jesus, not as BEING cursed at Calvary, but rather as BEING MADE the curse at Calvary.

This is parallel to a fundamental New Covenant truth, also established by Paul:

"For he hath made him to be sin for us, who knew no sin; that we might be made the righteousness of God in him." (2 Corinthians 5:21 KJV)

Jesus had never committed a sin, yet God made Him to be sin for us. Compare this to Galatians 3:13 in which God allowed Jesus to hang on a tree, thereby making Him into the curse for us. In one moment, the sinless One was viewed as sin (not as a sinner, but as having the sins of all sinners within Him), and then the curse that was to fall on mankind for the breaking of God's law was personified in that One who was carrying all of those sins.

The Curse of the Law

"Christ has redeemed us from the curse of the law," (Galatians 3:13) was a world-changing statement within itself. Not only did it declare Christ as redeemer from something other than sin, it stated that the law of God had a curse attached to it. I think the arguments that Paul would have fielded regarding that statement have changed somewhat over two millennia. In his day, he might have had to defend such a statement against those who felt that nothing could replace the law and that faith in Christ was not enough to secure salvation. In our day, I think his defense would be against those who would take him to task for saying there is a curse attached to the law at all!

We tend to view the Law of Moses as the model for what God looks like, sounds like, acts like, and expects. If we want to live right, we study the law. If we want our kids to understand morality, we hang the Ten Commandments in their school hallways. If the school board rules against hanging the Ten Commandments, we cry discrimination and persecution and blog about the fall of modern society and the rise of heathenism. Perhaps our exaltation of the law is due to our ignorance of the curse that was inexorably attached to it.

From the earliest days of their wilderness journey, Israel saw the by-products of Mosaic Law. Much could be written of the deaths and judgments meted out upon their murmuring, complaining, sinning and rebellion. By the time they arrived at the banks of the Jordan, after nearly forty years of wandering around the same mountain, they have an inbred affinity to seeing the law as the bringer of the curse more than the bringer of the blessing.

Upon their crossing of the Jordan River into the Promised Land, the Israelites had received strict instructions on what to do on the very first day of their crossing, and it involved an intricate ceremony regarding the blessings and cursings of the law.

> "And it shall be, on the day when you cross over the Jordan to the land which the LORD your God is giving you, that you shall set up for yourselves large stones, and whitewash them with lime. You shall write on them all the words of this law, when you have crossed over, that you may enter the land which the LORD your God is giving you, 'a land flowing with milk and honey,' just as the LORD God of your fathers promised you. Therefore it shall be, when you have crossed over the Jordan, that on Mount Ebal you shall set up these stones, which I command you today, and you shall whitewash them with lime. And there you shall build an altar to the LORD your God, an altar of stones; you shall not use an iron tool on them. You shall build with whole stones the altar of the LORD your God, and offer burnt offerings on it to the LORD your God. You shall offer peace offerings, and shall eat there, and rejoice before the LORD your God. And you shall write very plainly on the stones all the words of this law." (Deuteronomy 27:2-8)

Their first responsibility was to find large stones, whitewash them and then write the law upon them. The requirement of "stones" speaks to the method of the giving of the Ten Commandments (written on stone), and the size of the stones is to accommodate the size of the law (for in its entirety, it is more than just the Ten Commandments).

The act of whitewashing was obviously performed to make the markings or writings stand out against the harsh color of the stone, but I think it speaks to something deeper about how the law functions. There is no power in the law to permanently change someone, thus to put on the law as a covering or a way of life, is to put it on as a whitewashed stone. The whitewash may impress someone, giving the illusion of cleanliness, but the stone holds no life within it, which is why Jesus contrasted a stone with bread in Luke 11:11. He also made a further allusion to this passage in a conversation with the "ultimate law-keepers," the Pharisees.

> *"Woe to you, scribes and Pharisees, hypocrites! For you are like white-washed tombs which indeed appear beautiful outwardly, but inside are full of dead men's bones and all uncleanness."* (Matthew 23:27)

To whitewash the outside of a tomb is to bring beauty to that which holds none. The law was placed over whitewash because all it could do was effect the outside of a man, though his insides were "all uncleanness."

Gerizim and Ebal

Once the Israelites had whitewashed the stones and written the law on them, they were to set them up on Mount Ebal. This giant mountain stood near its twin, Gerizim, comprising the two highest peaks of an east to west mountain range, towering nearly one thousand feet above the town of Shechem. The word Ebal means "stone" or "bare mountain" in Hebrew, and the mountain is made of limestone rock. Note that the stones that contained the law were to be set on a mountain named "stone." The typologies are thick, as God is showing us the rigid, never-changing, coldness of the law.

> *"These shall stand on Mount Gerizim to bless the people, when you have crossed over the Jordan: Simeon, Levi, Judah, Issachar, Joseph, and Benjamin; and these shall stand on Mount Ebal to curse: Reuben, Gad, Asher, Zebulun, Dan, and Naphtali."* (Deuteronomy 27:12, 13)

The twelve tribes of Israel were to split, with six tribes standing on Gerizim and the other six standing on Ebal. The whitewashed stone bearing the law was to stand with the group on Ebal. The group on Gerizim was to pronounce the blessings and the group on Ebal, the curses. There are interesting shadows in this story that teach us some remarkable New Covenant substance. Remember, the volume of the book was written about Jesus, so looking for Him in stories like this is sanctioned exegesis.

The mountain from which the blessings were pronounced was named Gerizim, meaning "the cutting off." Contrast this to Ebal, which means "stone" and then identify Jesus in the setting. The law was written on a stone and placed on Ebal, and Paul said the Law of Moses was "written and engraved on stone" (2 Corinthians 3:7), thus Ebal becomes an obvious picture of the law. John declared the law was given by Moses, but grace and truth came by Jesus (John 1:17), thus we can conclude the opposite mountain could represent Christ. No twisting of scripture is necessary in order to find out if a "cutting off" (Gerizim) took place in Jesus.

> *"He was taken from prison and from judgment, and who will declare His generation? For He was **cut off** from the land of the living; for the transgressions of My people He was stricken."* (Isaiah 53:8)

> *"In Him you were also circumcised with the circumcision made without hands, by putting off the body of the sins of the flesh, by the circumcision of Christ."* (Colossians 2:11)

The former text, states clearly that Jesus was cut off from the living, while the latter text speaks of "the circumcision of Christ." This circumcision is not referring to a literal, physical circumcision of Jesus, for it is one "made without hands." Jesus was cut off in His death in the same way the foreskin is cut off in circumcision. From the time of Abraham forward, the circumcision demanded of all Israelites pointed to the reality of Christ's death, His "cutting off."

His cutting off results in our never being cut off or cut out of the heavenly will! From Gerizim, which identifies with the cutting off, we have the pronouncement of blessings. Contrast that with Ebal, a rocky, craggy home for the law, from which the curses are pronounced. One mountain speaks of God's grace and the other speaks of the law; blessings come from grace and curses come from law. This is one explanation for Paul saying, "Christ has redeemed us from the curse of the law."

The Place of the Altar

"And there you shall build an altar to the LORD your God, an altar of stones; you shall not use an iron tool on them." (Deuteronomy 27:5)

[It is possible that the stones, upon which the law was to be written, were the same stones that were to constitute the altar built on Ebal.] Either way, we can be sure that the stones were to have no tool used on them (no works of man's hands could shape the law or establish the place of sacrifice), and that the altar was not to be on Gerizim, but rather on Ebal.

It makes more sense to establish the altar on the mountain of "cutting off," where the blessings are pronounced, until you consider, again, that all things point to Jesus. His death was a sacrificial death, meaning that Calvary was an altar. Just as the evening sacrifice was happening in the temple at 3 pm, Jesus was giving up the ghost on the cross as the Lamb of God. This hanging on a tree made Jesus "cursed," so "that the blessing of Abraham might come upon the Gentiles in Christ Jesus" (Galatians 3:14).

The altar MUST be on Ebal because the curses pronounced there must be paid for. While the Israelites were sacrificing from that mountain to make recompense to God for the curse, Jesus is metaphorically sacrificed on that mount as those very curses. Because He was crucified at the point of the curse (Ebal), we can live in the place of the blessing (Gerizim).

"Neither on this mountain, nor in Jerusalem…"

Rather than the city of Jerusalem, Mount Gerizim is considered sacred to many Samaritans, as they believed this was the place God had chosen to build a holy temple. Their religious identity revolved around this place, as is evidenced in the conversation between Jesus and a Samaritan, the nameless Woman at the Well.

"The woman said to Him, "Sir, I perceive that You are a prophet. Our fathers worshiped on this mountain, and you Jews say that in Jerusalem is the place where one ought to worship." (John 4:19, 20)

Gerizim is commonly considered to be the mountain to which the woman is referring. Jesus counters by telling her that the time is coming when they will not worship God on any mountain, but rather they will worship Him in the dimension of the Spirit. This is prophetically speaking of a time (in which we live, under the New Covenant) when mankind could have an internal, personal relationship with God without traveling to a mountain, a holy city, or a temple. He isn't condemning her for viewing Gerizim as holy; He is simply expanding her horizons.

I share this passage in order to show you the chasm that existed between Jew and Samaritan, and to show how damaging the law can be when used for righteousness. The battle between Jews and Samaritans is ancient, but the long and short of their rift goes back to around 722 B.C. when Assyria conquered the northern kingdom of Israel (Judah had split into its own nation in the south some years earlier). 2 Kings 17 tells of the invading Assyrians bringing in foreign gods and Gentile pilgrims from all over. Over time, the remaining Israelites began to worship the strange gods along with God, and they mixed marriages with the Gentiles.

Over one hundred years later, the southern kingdom of Judah fell to the Babylonians. Several decades after this, thousands of Jews were allowed to return to their homeland and begin rebuilding the walls of Jerusalem. The inhabitants of the northern kingdom were second and third generation Samaritans, mixed peoples of Jewish and Gentile lineage, and they violently opposed the repatriation of Jerusalem. While the Samaritans did not want an entirely Jewish Jerusalem, the Jews disliked the mixed blooded Samaritans who had a history of serving strange gods. As history tells us, this type of racial discrimination tends to harden over the centuries.

It was this old paradigm of hate that was a source of disgust for Jesus, as He would aim certain parables and actions around removing the racial barrier. Whether it is His insistence at traveling through Samaria in John 4:4 (no Jew went through Samaria who didn't have to!), or His famous story of the Good

Samaritan in Luke 10, Jesus was always shocking in His ability to paint people in a positive light when others felt negative towards them.

Was Jesus elevating the Samaritans above the Jews? Absolutely not, but He was elevating them back to the same level as the Jews, in spite of their rather shady past. While the Jews trusted the Law of Moses for their righteousness and looked down on others who could not boast of such a "pure" pedigree, Jesus plays the role of Gerizim, showing grace to those who were dwelling on the "wrong" mountain.

The law had worked wrath in the heart of the Israelites (Romans 4:15), and those who found their altar and their law firmly entrenched on Ebal had no mercy for those who worshipped at Gerizim. According to many ancient rabbinical sources, in order to convert to Judaism, a Samaritan was required to renounce his belief in the sanctity of Mount Gerizim. This is paramount to someone renouncing his belief in a God who freely blesses by grace and then turning to a performance based religion, dependent upon works and effort. It is like experiencing the joy and freedom of knowing Jesus through relationship and then turning to some other concept of God, void of His personal presence. The author of Hebrews warned the Jews that had come out of Judaism and into righteousness by faith of doing this.

> *"Of how much worse punishment, do you suppose, will he be thought worthy who has trampled the Son of God underfoot, counted the blood of the covenant by which he was sanctified a common thing, and insulted the Spirit of grace?"* (Hebrews 10:29)

To insult the Spirit of grace is to insult that which flows from Gerizim in favor of going back to the law of Ebal. Further in the chapter, the author continues:

> *"'Now the just shall live by faith; but if anyone draws back, My soul has no pleasure in him.' But we are not of those who draw back to perdition, but of those who believe to the saving of the soul."* (Hebrews 10:38, 39)

Roll Call

When you look at the division of the tribes on these two mountains, the most obvious one is mathematical, as there are six tribes on each. But a closer look at the names will reveal an apparent randomness to the selections. I personally see no room for mindless randomness in the Bible, as it is not a history book simply listing dates and names; but it is a book of shadows and substance. The shadows of the Old Testament lead to the substance of the New, and while I admit one can put too much stock in numerology and typology, these exist for a reason and should at least be examined.

First, we must acknowledge the presence of Joseph among the tribes and the absence of the tribes of Mannaseh and Ephraim. Joseph is rarely listed as a tribe since his sons, Mannaseh and Ephraim, were given the inheritance of full sonship by their grandfather Jacob (Genesis 48:5). Writings often refer to the "family of Joseph," rather than the "tribe of Joseph." Levi, as well, is not always listed among the tribes due to its lack of receiving a land inheritance (no land was needed since Levi was the tribe of the priesthood), thus many lists will exclude both Joseph and Levi and still have twelve members.

In this instance of listing the twelve tribes, Joseph and Levi are included with no real explanation as to why. I believe this lends itself to the idea that God has a purpose in both the order of the names listed, and to which mountain they are standing on. In other words, to find a solution, we may have to dig a bit deeper.

Beginning in Genesis 29:32, the record of the birth order of each of the tribal heads of Israel is recorded. The following list shows the chronological order, from oldest to youngest, of the twelve tribes, along with their mother's name and her relation to Jacob, their father:

Reuben – son of Leah, wife of Jacob
Simeon – son of Leah
Levi – son of Leah
Judah – son of Leah
Dan – son of Bilhah, servant of Jacob's wife, Rachel
Naphtali – son of Bilhah
Gad – son of Zilpah, servant of Jacob's wife, Leah
Asher – son of Zilpah

Issachar – son of Leah
Zebulun – son of Leah
Joseph – son of Rachel
Benjamin – son of Rachel

Notice in the previous list that Leah had six sons for Jacob while his other wife Rachel had two. Both women had servants, or slaves, who also bore two children apiece for Jacob. Now look at the order they are listed on both mountains:

Gerizim	Ebal
Simeon	Reuben
Levi	Gad
Judah	Asher
Issachar	Zebulun
Joseph	Dan
Benjamin	Naphtali

You can see that they are not listed in order of birth, as this would have had Reuben, Dan and Naphtali on Gerizim, since they were born first, fifth and sixth respectively. Thus, at first glance, the listing of these tribes seems a bit haphazard. But go back and look at the birth mother for each child, and you see something of interest. Everyone listed on Mt. Gerizim was the son of one of Jacob's two wives, Leah and Rachel. Four of the six tribes on Mt. Ebal are sons of the slave women, Bilhah and Zilpah. It would be easy to proclaim the mountain of blessing as holding those born in the covenant of marriage, while the curse is for those born of the slave, but for there to be a correlating typology, shouldn't all six on Ebal have the same in common? Shouldn't they ALL be born of the slave women? Obviously, Reuben and Zebulun were not.

The Curse of the Firstborn

From his deathbed, Jacob gathers his sons together to tell them "what shall befall you in the last days" (Genesis 49:1). This was an anticipated moment in any Jewish household, as the patriarch could pronounce any number of blessings on his sons. As was custom, Jacob starts with his eldest, Reuben.

"Unstable as water, you shall not excel, because you went up to your father's bed; then you defiled it – he went up to my couch." (Genesis 49:4)

Following this rebuke of Reuben, Jacob moves on to blessing his other sons, effectively denying an extra blessing to Reuben, who deserves it as Jacob's firstborn. This reference to the defilement of his father's bed speaks back to an incident that gets nearly no play on the stage of the Bible.

"And it happened, when Israel dwelt in that land, that Reuben went and lay with Bilhah his father's concubine; and Israel heard about it." (Genesis 35:22)

That is all we learn! Apparently no child was born of this incident, and perhaps Jacob said and did nothing when he learned of it. But when the time came to bless his son, Jacob reminded him and everyone present of the incident, and showed his displeasure by denying him the blessing. Not only is there a blessing denied, but there is a curse pronounced. Though the word "curse" is not used, "you shall not excel," is a curse within itself! Reuben lived the remainder of his life knowing that he could never excel in life, due to the failure in his youth.

Many have taken the story of Reuben's curse to declare a general curse on all firstborn children. They couple this with Joshua's prophecy of Joshua 6:26, in which he puts a curse on the man that tries to rebuild the city of Jericho. The curse promised the death of the man's firstborn son upon the laying of the foundation. What people often miss in quoting this is that the man was also supposed to lose his youngest son when he set up the city gates. They also ignore that this curse was fulfilled in 1 Kings 16:34, when Hiel the Bethelite lost his firstborn and his youngest when he rebuilt Jericho.

The idea of the "Curse of Reuben" has extended into the world of secular literature. The popular British writer Rudyard Kipling used the expression, *"The curse of Reuben holds us till an alien turf enfolds us,"* in his work *Gentleman Rankers.*[1] However widespread the thought might be, there is no scriptural evidence to support a doctrine of the firstborn curse. Reuben's curse to "not excel" was certainly carried on to the families within his tribe, as the prophecies were to deal with generations of families born into each tribe. But to take that curse and apply it to all firstborn children makes no sense, since God placed no such curse on the remaining tribes, or on anyone outside the tribe of Reuben for that matter.

All previous points aside, what matters most is that God provided a way for the generations of children crushed beneath the curse of their forefather to have a way out. By placing the tribe of Reuben on Ebal, the place of the curse, where an altar was set up to pay for that curse, God was providing redemption. Because Jesus is crucified as the curse, those of Reuben can be blessed.

In everyday terminology, there is no such thing as a "firstborn curse" or a "generational curse" to those who are in Christ Jesus, for He was made to be the curse at Calvary, and all of us who were crushed beneath a mountain of law can now know that we are free!

What about Zebulun?

The fact remains that there is still one unaccounted for member of the congregation on Ebal. We can see why Reuben belongs there, to break the curse of failure, but what about the other son of Leah? Zebulun was a son born within the covenant of marriage, with no abject failure recorded in scripture, so why his inclusion with these others?

At first glance, the answer is not very clear, and I'll admit, even with digging it could be considered hard to find. I personally think Zebulun is on Ebal for more than to just even out the numbers, but I do think his "number" has a lot to do with it.

Leah bore Jacob six sons: Reuben, Simeon, Levi, Judah, Issachar and Zebulun. In Hebrew numerology, as well as many Christian sources, the number six denotes "evil," or "man," (in some secular sources it even denotes "religious perfection"). These are tied to the Biblical uses for "six," such as man being created on the sixth day; man working only six days of the week and resting on the seventh; six different words in the Bible being used for the word "man" and the number of the beast in Revelation adding up to 666.

Perhaps the issue is not found in the number of sons that Leah bore for Jacob, but rather in the fact that her sixth son, Zebulun, is told to stand on Mount Ebal.

As the sixth, Zebulun comes to represent man in his imperfection, short of the perfection found in God. Zebulun takes his place beneath the law, for that is the highest form of righteousness that man can hope to achieve without the grace of God. By dwelling on Ebal, where the altar represents the cross, he represents mankind at the foot of Calvary, where the ground is level and all of the guilty are paid for.

It is also worth noting what the names of the tribes mean in the Hebrew language, and [I don't wish to stretch the illustration past the breaking point but] it is interesting to see what these meanings relate when the names are put together. As for the congregation on Gerizim, which pronounce the blessing, their names, when put in the order in which they appear, do have a particularly fascinating proclamation:

Simeon ("hearing"), Levi ("attached" or "joined"), Judah ("praise"), Issachar ("he will bring reward"), Joseph ("let him add") and Benjamin ("son of the right hand"). These could string together and say, "When your hearing (of Him) is attached to your praise (of Him), He will bring a reward by adding (to you) the Son of His right hand (Jesus)." I am not advocating a dedication to numerology and to the meanings of names, but the correlation is both interesting and fascinating!

"Amen" to the Curse?

The Levites (the tribe of the priesthood) were to read aloud "all the words of this law very plainly" (Deuteronomy 27:8). The words they were to speak were divided into two promises: curses and blessings. They started with the curses.

> "Cursed is the one who makes a carved or molded image, an abomination to the LORD, the work of the hands of the craftsman, and sets it up in secret.' And all the people shall answer and say, 'Amen!'" (Deuteronomy 27:15)

I will not go through every one of the curses (there are twelve of them in Deuteronomy 27), but I do want to show you the nature of them. They consist of a command with a corresponding curse to the one who disobeys the command. In this case, there is a curse on someone who commits the abomination of carving or molding an image. [They continue on through curses for mistreating one's parents, moving one's neighbor's property line, abusing the handicapped, committing incest, etc.] Without listing all of them, look for one common ending in each verse.

> *"Cursed is the one who treats his father or his mother with contempt.' And all the people shall say, 'Amen!'"* (Deuteronomy 27:16)

> *"Cursed is the one who moves his neighbor's landmark.' And all the people shall say, "Amen!'"* (Deuteronomy 27:17)

> *"Cursed is the one'...And all the people shall say, 'Amen!'"* (Deuteronomy 27:15-26)

No matter the curse, the people, in unison, always declare "Amen!" The word "amen" did not hold the same meaning for a Hebrew that it seems to hold now in the American church. We use the word to denote our firm agreement with something that we like. Someone will say, "It sure is a beautiful day," and we will respond, "Amen." We are agreeing that the day is beautiful. To the Hebrew, this would have made no sense.

The word 'amen' was used as a seal, or a claim. When you declared 'amen,' you were putting your seal of approval on a statement and claiming it as your own. Rabbinical tradition states that whatever Heaven has to offer is procured by the "Amen!" This was a statement of affirmation that was more binding than a simple nod of the head or a grunt of agreement. The "amen" was often seen as on par with the seal of a king on a royal document.

Unfortunately, we have grown accustomed to hearing "Amen!" at the most inopportune moments in the modern church. Preachers will declare an angry God that is full of fury and rage over a world full of sin and threaten the congregation with judgment and hell, and the sound of "Amen!" will sound forth from the sanctuary. Do we realize what we are placing our approval upon? Have we stopped to consider that when we "Amen," we are declaring these things to be? I'm not insinuating that by our saying it, God is forced to do it, or to become it, but why should we live beneath this guilt and condemnation when we don't have to? Why make God look bad, when He has done so much to show that He is good?

"Amen!" to the Good Stuff

Knowing what "amen" means, we must consider why the Hebrews would say it at the end of each curse. Why put your seal of approval on the curses? Our initial assumption is that they did it because that was their universal answer, whether the statement was a curse or a blessing. To find out if this is true, let's move past the curses listed in Chapter 27 and on into the blessings of Chapter 28.

> *"Blessed shall you be in the city, and blessed shall you be in the country."* (Deuteronomy 28:3)

> *"Blessed shall be the fruit of your body, the produce of your ground and the increase of your cattle and the offspring of your flocks."* (Deuteronomy 28:4)

After only two blessings, we notice the absence of the "amen." It continues this way on through all of the blessings of obedience through Verse 14. Why no "amen" to the good stuff?

Revelation 3:14 may hold part of the answer as the angel to the church of the Laodiceans says, "These things says the Amen, the Faithful and True Witness, the Beginning of the creation of God." Jesus is here identified as the Amen, personifying what had once been only a declaration. Having been made a curse on our behalf, Jesus takes it upon Himself to be the seal of approval to all of Heaven's goodness. Paul stated it this way:

> *"For all the promises of God in Him are Yes, and in Him Amen, to the glory of God through us."* (2 Corinthians 1:20)

All of God's promises are available to us through Jesus, who IS the Amen! When we declare "Amen!" we are taking the benefits afforded to us by the finished work of Christ. In actuality, we are declaring "Jesus!" with our "amen." Perhaps the reason the children of Israel could only say "amen" to the curses at Gerizim and Ebal was because the curses were the only ones they could guarantee! Without the help and aid of the Holy Spirit in their hearts, they could never expect to live to a high enough standard to warrant the blessings.

While we may fail from time to time in our walk with the Lord, we have the wonderful Holy Spirit inside to guide us into all truth. Because of Christ's finished work in being made the curse on our behalf, all of the promises of God are ours. We can say "Amen!" to those promises and appropriate heaven's blessings into our lives. We need not fear our own inability, thinking we won't live good enough to merit His grace, for it can only be provided by what the Amen has done on our behalf. This sets us free to simply live, with no fear of a firstborn curse, a generational curse or any other curse. We are "curse free" because Jesus has been our substitute!

He Was Cursed So That Abraham's Blessing Might Land on You!

"That the blessing of Abraham might come upon the Gentiles in Christ Jesus, that we might receive the promise of the Spirit through faith." (Galatians 3:14)

Please don't forget the reason that Jesus was made to be the curse. It was so "that the blessing of Abraham might come upon the Gentiles." We are those Gentiles, outside of the children of Israel, upon whom the original blessing of Abraham has been bestowed. Where a Jew identified with Abraham and his blessing through heritage and obedience, we are ushered into that blessing through our identification with the slain Lamb, Jesus Christ. In Him we have received the endless presence of the Holy Spirit, activated by our faith.

Simply believe that Jesus was made to be all the Word says that He was, and prepare yourself for the free favors of God. Your destiny is to live in all the goodness that Abraham had, which came by his faith and not by his works. As we proceed, we will look intently into the covenant benefits he enjoyed so we can find out what to expect in our lives. We will also take his covenant and lay it on top of the one that Jesus cut at the cross to find out what was really happening in both. In the meantime, let's rest together in the glorious knowledge that Jesus took whatever it was that we had coming to us by our works, and gave us what He had coming by His perfection. He was cursed so the whole world could be blessed. Now THAT is good news!

Endnote

1. Rudyard Kipling, *Gentleman Rankers* (New York, NY: Alfred A. Knopf a division of Random House, Inc, 2007), 44.

Chapter 4

Did God forsake His Own Son?

I have never been a fan of the phrase, "God-forsaken." People often use it to describe the hopelessness of a person or a place. I suppose I originally disliked it because I was raised to never use the word "God" in front of, or behind, any other word that wasn't praise, as this was considered taking the Lord's name in vain. As I grow older in years, and also in the faith, I have come to dislike the phrase on principle.

My God doesn't forsake anyone, anytime, for any reason.

Or does He?

Within the message of grace we hear the phrase (and I have used it as well), "God forsook Jesus so that He will never forsake you." This sounds good because it makes us feel as if we have the security of His presence forever. However, we have that security whether the statement is true or not, for Deuteronomy 31:6 declares, *"He will not leave you nor forsake you,"* and Hebrews 13:5 backs it up as a New Covenant promise as well. In neither scripture is the promise contingent on Jesus being forsaken so that we never will be.

As we learned in the previous chapter, all of our promises come to us through Jesus (2 Corinthians 1:20). More specifically, everything we have, or have access to through Jesus, is made available because of His death, burial and resurrection. The cross was the place where God's work was finished, thus our appropriation of the provisions of that finished work will always come through the conduit of Calvary. If we have the promise that we will not be forsaken, we can be sure that it, along with everything else, is ours because of Jesus.

I'm fine with the idea that God forsook Jesus so that He will not forsake me, if scripture backs it up. But if scripture does not support this idea, it runs dangerously close to us making our Father look bad, as no parent takes kindly to the accusation of child abandonment! In our task of making our Father look as good, as we know He is, answering the following question becomes paramount:

"Did God forsake His own Son?"

The question comes from an incident that occurred on the cross, when Jesus was offering Himself as the sacrifice for the sin of the world. During the ninth hour of the day on the Jewish clock (3:00 pm, Roman time), after three hours of mid-day darkness, Jesus, "cried out with a loud voice, saying, 'Eloi, Eloi, lama sabachthani?' Which is translated, 'My God, My God, why have You forsaken Me?'" (Mark 15:34).

The fact that Jesus asked God why He had forsaken Him has actually kept some from believing on Jesus. They view the statement as evidence that Jesus was taken off guard at the cross, and that He was not fully aware of what was happening. If this be the case, then one might conclude that Jesus was confused as to what was happening to Him. Or one could argue that Jesus became disillusioned at Calvary, having been fully persuaded of what He was doing until God up and left Him. Someone could even make the claim that on the cross, Jesus realized He was just a man, not the Son of God, and that He stopped calling God, "Father," and resorted to calling Him, "God," just like any other man. These arguments can be made, but I believe they are patently wrong!

Don't forget what we discussed earlier: the crowd at Calvary *thought* that what they were seeing at the Crucifixion was God cursing Jesus for claiming to be one with Him. This is why Isaiah said they esteemed Him as "smitten of God" (Isaiah 53:4). While Jesus' statement in Mark 15:34 may be confusing to us, I propose that He did not say it because *He* was confused, disillusioned or disappointed. He did not even say it to further confuse an already confused crowd. Jesus proclaimed "Why have You forsaken me?" to *clear up their confusion!*

The Crowd at the Cross

The Gospels of Matthew and Mark both include Jesus' question about being forsaken while on the cross; Luke and John do not. For purposes of ascertaining why Jesus would make such a remark, let's look at some context leading into this statement. We will use Mark's version of the story.

> *"And those who passed by blasphemed Him, wagging their heads and saying, "Aha! You who destroy the temple and build it in three days, save Yourself, and come down from the cross!"* (Mark 15:29, 30)

What the crowd doesn't realize (remember, they are convinced He is being cursed for blasphemy), is that an important reason that Jesus is hanging on the cross is because of their transgressions (Isaiah 53:5). If He saves Himself and comes down from the cross, no one else can be saved! His hanging is their hanging. His death is their death.

This verse also reveals an important fact about the ability of the crowd to misunderstand things they had both seen and heard. They thought that Jesus was speaking of the literal temple when He said, in John 2:19, "Destroy this temple, and in three days I will raise it up." On the other side of the cross, we know that He was obviously speaking of the temple of His body.

> *"Likewise the chief priests also, mocking among themselves with the scribes, said, "He saved others; Himself He cannot save."* (Mark 15:31)

The sarcasm is thick in these words of the religious leaders. They have disdained Jesus during His entire earthly ministry for His public rebukes of them and their ways (Matthew 23:13-36). Their statement regarding Him "saving others," is no doubt a literal reference to the many folk who were healed, fed and resurrected during His ministry. But the statement, coupled with the follow-up "Himself He cannot save," tends to indicate that they were actually mocking those who claimed any sort of salvation at the hands of this man. How could you claim He had really "saved" you, if He couldn't even "save" Himself?

"Let the Christ, the King of Israel, descend now from the cross, that we may see and believe.' Even those who were crucified with Him reviled Him." (Mark 15:32)

The command from the crowd, and from the criminals hanging on either side, is obviously a heartless mockery of the sign that hung above His head, declaring Him to be the "King of the Jews." They demand to see so that they might believe, which had always been Israel's way. If God moved, then they believed. But Jesus was establishing a higher form of faith. His version of justification would not be established upon what they can see, but rather on whether or not they could believe what they heard the Word of God say. This is why Paul stated that "faith comes by hearing, and hearing by the word of God" (Romans 10:17).

"Now when the sixth hour had come, there was darkness over the whole land until the ninth hour." (Mark 15:33)

At high noon (the sixth hour to a Jew), the sky went dark, covering the land until 3:00 pm. We will deal with what happened during this three hour period of darkness in a later chapter, so for now, let's move on.

"Eloi, Eloi..." What?

"And at the ninth hour Jesus cried out with a loud voice, saying, 'Eloi, Eloi, lama sabachtani?' which is translated, 'My God, My God, why have You forsaken Me?'" (Mark 15:34)

As we mentioned earlier, only Matthew and Mark record this statement by Jesus. What is of further interest is that both writers include the Hebrew translation of what Jesus said as well. Please note that these Gospels were written in Greek, the common language for literature in the world of that day. To include a phrase in Hebrew was to draw special emphasis on that phrase above all others, since Jesus would have said a lot of things in Hebrew while on earth. Considering He was ministering in Palestine, to Jews, much of His day-to-day teachings would have been conducted in their native tongue. The point being: Why include the Hebrew translation here, but not every time Jesus spoke?

The usage of Hebrew words in the midst of Greek writing is not isolated to the cross. When Jesus is called to the home of Jairus, to heal his twelve year old daughter, Jesus takes her by the hand and says, "'Talitha, cumi,' which is, being interpreted, 'Damsel, I say unto thee, arise'" (Mark 5:41). Matthew and Luke included this story in their Gospels, yet neither used the literal Hebrew words. Does this indicate that Jesus didn't really say it? No, it simply lends credence to the idea that Mark liked to use the Hebrew with the Greek. (Mark does it again, in Mark 7:34, when Jesus heals a deaf and dumb man, using the word, "Ephphatha," which means "be opened." This story appears in Mark's Gospel only.)

That calls special attention to Matthew's usage of the Hebrew in the midst of Greek writing. Since only Matthew and Mark's versions of the crucifixion include this statement by Jesus, and Matthew is NOT prone to including the Hebrew with the Greek, I can't help but conclude that this is done by direction of the Spirit, more than just due to the author's style.

It is not necessary to try and figure out what "Eloi, Eloi, lama sabachtani" means, since the verse explains the translation to be "My God, My God, why have You forsaken Me?" That does not, however, explain why the Hebrew phrase exists in our translation. This forces us to consider something that many modern readers forget when they are reading the Bible.

The Bible is certainly the inspired Word of God, and everything in it is beneficial for life and living. As much as the Bible is *for* us, it was not written *to* us. It contains the story of man and his fall (Adam), followed by God's plan for restoring man back to Himself (we are certainly skipping many important details with that synopsis), and ultimately, His moving into mankind to live out of him. The Old Testament (Torah) was given to Israel for the purpose of dividing mankind and separating out a holy people through whom the Messiah could enter the world. The Word (Jesus) became flesh in the Gospels and finished the work of redeeming mankind. Then, in the body of the New Testament, God introduces us to a joint life between heaven and earth, with God taking up residence within the man whom He had lost in the beginning.

Keeping that in mind, picture Jesus hanging on the cross, speaking to the crowd that is responsible for His crucifixion. *They* are the intended audience of the Old Testament. *They* are the holy people that were set aside to be the womb of the One they are murdering. In order to get a message across to them, He must speak their language, and in order for the modern audience to know why He is saying it, and to whom He is saying it, it is specifically included in the language in which He said it. In other words, *these words are written in Hebrew so that we would know that Jesus was specifically pointing at something only a Jew would understand.*

Many people in the crowd at Calvary were well-versed in the Torah. They heard readings from it every Sabbath day when they attended their local synagogue. The more learned among them, such as the scribes and the Pharisees, had large portions of it memorized, and took great pride in being able to quote extended passages. Among the more famous and widely used portions of the Torah, was the great book of Psalms. These Psalms constituted the longest book of the sacred writings, and was also the songbook of the Hebrew people.

With a crowd bent on blood and execution, convinced that God is cursing this confused carpenter for claiming equality with heaven, Jesus speaks loud and clear to them, pointing those who will hear it, to the exact chapter and verse they need in order to see the real reason for His death. His statement would have been a familiar one, much like the opening lines to a song we have heard many times before. Just a few words into the melody, and we begin to sing along. Jesus is quoting both their book and their song:

> *"My God, My God, why have You forsaken Me? Why are You so far from helping Me, and from the words of My groaning?"* (Psalm 22:1)

Jesus was not crying out in confusion! He was quoting from the book of Psalms, pointing His audience to a specific chapter. He wanted the crowd that day, and all who would ever hear of His dying words, to know why He was on that cross. He did not cry out because He believed that God was forsaking Him, but He did so because He believed the Jews were missing why He was hanging there. He knew they would interpret His death on a tree as a curse of God. He knew Isaiah 53:4 that said, "We did esteem Him smitten of God." He wanted to steer them, not toward the idea of God turning His back on His Son, but toward the revelation that was available in their own book. Even in death, the Savior is trying to save. He is sending them back to the Bible, so they would go home and find the chapter that starts with His cry.

Go and Learn What it Means

Jesus was fond of pointing His audience to things written in the Old Testament. Whether He was giving a direct quote ("as it is written..."), or giving a general reference ("you have heard it has been said..."), He was often using the text. Sometimes, He would make a reference and then send His audience home to search it out, like spiritual homework. Note the following incident, in which Jesus is found sharing a meal with "tax collectors and sinners":

> *"And when the Pharisees saw it, they said to His disciples, 'Why does your Teacher eat with tax collectors and sinners?' When Jesus heard that, He said to them, 'Those who are well have no need of a physician, but those who are sick. But go and learn what this means: 'I desire mercy and not sacrifice.' For I did not come to call the righteous, but sinners, to repentance.'"* (Matthew 9:13)

Notice that Jesus provides a quote, but doesn't cite that quote. In fact, He doesn't even specify that it is a quote. He knows that the Pharisees have knowledge of the scriptures, so He sees no need to provide specifics, only a roadmap.

If they were to take Him up on the challenge, they would arrive at Hosea 6:6, which states, "For I desire mercy and not sacrifice, and the knowledge of God more than burnt offerings." He doesn't question whether or not they know where the passage is located, but rather, whether or not they have even an elementary knowledge of what it means. This is a prime example of Jesus simply stating the verse, and allowing the people to do the research. Jesus refrained from simply giving them the answers because He wanted them to know the highest honor of finding revelation within the scriptures. That honor is ours as well, as Proverbs declares, "It is the glory of God to conceal a matter, but the glory of kings is to search out a matter" (Proverbs 25:2).

Unfortunately, the Pharisees either ignored His advice regarding Hosea, or they studied it and came to the wrong conclusion. Three chapters later, when addressing an accusation of His disciples breaking the Sabbath law, Jesus brings them back to their homework:

"Yet I say to you that in this place there is One greater than the temple. But if you had known what this means, 'I desire mercy and not sacrifice,' you would not have condemned the guiltless. For the Son of Man is Lord even of the Sabbath." (Matthew 12:6-8)

These two quotes fall within the same book, and are spoken to the same audience, yet at different times. It seems impossible for it to be random coincidence that Jesus would quote the same passage twice. He has directed them to study a specific scripture in order to determine why He acts the way He does. When they fail to understand that scripture, they come to a wrong conclusion, and make a decision based upon bad information, instead of one based upon truth.

At the cross, Jesus knows that the crowd is coming to a conclusion based upon bad information. They know what is supposed to happen to some random person based upon the death description of Isaiah 53. But Isaiah 53 is not person-specific. It does not indicate who is dying, only why he is dying. Jesus wants to clear the clouds of confusion by leading them to the proper place in order to use the context for a revelation of truth.

It is reasonable to assume that if Christ's own disciples had instant recall of many scriptures, then the average Israelite at Calvary would have similar knowledge. The disciples were not trained in great universities with backgrounds in theology. They were fishermen and tax-collectors. While I assume their knowledge of the Torah was more extensive than the average Christian's knowledge of the Bible (due to the fact that the Torah was probably the only text that most of them ever heard read aloud), they were far from scholarly.

An example of the disciples' ability to recall facts from the scriptures they had heard is found in the story of Christ cleansing the temple.

"And he said to those who sold doves, 'Take these things away! Do not make My Father's house a house of merchandise!' Then His disciples remembered that it was written, 'Zeal for Your house has eaten Me up.'" (John 2:16, 17)

When the disciples saw what Jesus was doing, they remembered Psalm 69, in which the prophecy of the event was contained. There is no indication that they had to go to their homes or synagogues to figure this out. Due to the Psalms being a part of their daily lives, it was simply common knowledge.

If the disciples knew Psalm 69, it is reasonable to assume they may have known Psalm 22. Also, if they knew Psalm 22, we can further assume that a majority of the everyday man on the street would have known it as well. Jesus' use of an Old Covenant song from Calvary should not be looked at as an obscure reference which could only be understood by the elite. He was speaking the language of the average Jew, and doing it from their popular songs!

It is important to note at this point, that though the disciples knew the scriptures, they did not always understand them. Just as the Pharisees knew Hosea 6:6, they obviously misunderstood its application. On Resurrection morning, Peter and John run into the tomb of Jesus and find only His grave clothes. Most modern translations state, "For as yet they did not know the Scripture, that He must rise again from the dead" (John 20:9). That would indicate that they didn't know the scripture existed that spoke of resurrection, which I don't believe is the case, since surely they knew Psalm 16:10, which is "the Scripture." That conclusion could only be reached by an improper translation of "did not know," from Greek. The phrase is better translated, "did not understand, or perceive," meaning that while they knew the verse, they did not understand it.

Not An Accusation, But Exoneration!

When Jesus cries out in question about God forsaking Him, it is not to accuse the Father of abandoning His Son. Rather than an accusation, Jesus uses the opportunity to exonerate the Father of the very thing the crowd is so sure He is involved in. Jesus is pointing His confused audience to the proper context of His crucifixion, confident that if they will study the 22nd Psalm, they will see parallels between two victims: the one in Psalm 22, and the one hanging on the cross.

"My God, My God, why have You forsaken Me?" (Mark 15:34)

I find this to be the only logical conclusion to this widely debated statement of Jesus. Any other interpretation has Jesus as disillusioned and confused, or as forsaken and forgotten. As we will find in our next chapter, there is even scriptural evidence against any interpretation of Jesus' statement that has God abandoning His Son in His hour of maximum need. This evidence leads me to believe that Jesus was not articulating confusion, but was rather pointing the way out of the confusion that the people were obviously under. He was dying to make all things new and to clear a path to a proper understanding of His Father.

Forsaken For A Moment

Some have used Isaiah 54:7 as a supporting verse for the idea that God forsook Jesus at the cross. See the verse, consider the context, and then read the next verse completely. This will help you determine the intended audience.

> *"For a mere moment I have forsaken you, but with great mercies I will gather you. With a little wrath I hid My face from you for a moment; but with everlasting kindness I will have mercy on you,' says the LORD, your Redeemer."* (Isaiah 54:7, 8)

This statement is being made to Israel, following the description of Christ's death in Chapter 53. It isn't Jesus who is the subject of the temporary forsaking in Verse 7, any more than it is Jesus who would need a Redeemer in Verse 8. Following the awesome price of the previous chapter, Israel is being encouraged with the promise that if it looks like God is mad at them and is forsaking them, they can rest assured that it is only for a moment, so that He can bring redemption by means of the Ultimate Sacrifice.

The warning of "forsaken for a moment," is not out in Israel's future, nor is it a part of her rocky present-day situation. The fulfillment of this scripture began in the period between the Testaments, when Malachi closed his book and before the events of the Book of Matthew began to unfold. That fulfillment was complete when Jesus became the sacrifice for Israel. The temporary darkness that Israel experienced due to captivity and the apparent silence of Heaven would be represented at Calvary by what Jesus would go through in a darkness of His own. This shows us that it was Israel, not Jesus, who should have expected to be forsaken.

Regarding the statement we used in the opening paragraphs of this chapter, "God forsook Jesus at the cross so that He will never forsake you," we now have a better idea: God temporarily forsook *Israel* to bring in His Messiah. Once He had His Messiah, He offered Him as a sacrifice for that nation, and for the entire earth outside of Israel. The wrath that Israel was experiencing was evidence that God had turned His face away. But, good news! God turning His face from *Israel* allowed Him to turn it toward His Son. Calvary was not God abandoning Jesus, Calvary was God abandoning having to deal with only one nation (Israel) in favor of dealing with the whole of humanity! We have a blessed assurance that God is not forsaking men or nations, and He is not turning away with even "a little wrath!"

Soak that last paragraph into your spirit for I know it can press against old mindsets and ideologies. Consider the Finished Work of the cross as more than just an assault against sin. Consider that Calvary was a turning point, and that when God did finally turn His face back onto humanity, He did not consider one nation or people above another. He viewed Christ's sacrifice as the tearing down of a middle wall of partition (Ephesians 2:14) between the Jew and the Gentile, and as the end of a racial distinction ("There is neither Jew nor Greek...for you are all one in Christ Jesus" Galatians 3:28).

If this all seems like a bit much, have no fear. We will deal with the covenants and what was accomplished from that aspect in great detail in a later chapter. One step at a time, we are arriving at our intended destination.

The next, and obvious step, is to closely examine the text that Jesus quotes at Calvary. If He wanted that audience to read Psalm 22, it would do us a world of good to see why He did so, and what the intended audience would have found. The answers to what was really happening at the cross begin to emerge from the clouds of mystery and into the clear skies of revelation as we follow the path of study that Jesus so meticulously laid out.

Chapter 5

Psalm 22:
The Calvary Code

Before we embark on a closer look at the Psalm that Jesus directs His audience to from the cross, let us remember that though the Jews had the sacred scriptures, they could not always interpret when and where the prophecies were going to be fulfilled. We should use caution in bringing judgment on their lack of insight since we are viewing the proceedings from the other side of the cross. We have had centuries of revelation and insight (as well as the indwelling Holy Spirit, which they did not have), to show us truths about the Finished Work.

Just as Peter developed his thoughts about what happened at Calvary over time, much of the early church would do the same thing. Long before Peter connected the dots of New Covenant realities to Old Covenant prophecies, Philip the Evangelist was using Isaiah 53 to point out Jesus to the Ethiopian eunuch in Acts 8. This shows that revelation can arrive in waves and at different times to different people.

Jesus gives no specifics from the cross regarding where to find His quote, relying instead on the knowledge of the Psalms held by the majority of those present. When, and if, they found the scripture He was quoting, they could read the remainder of the text and find things so jarring and shocking that it would appear the body of the Psalm was written *after* Jesus died on the cross. Psalm 22 is so spot-on that it's like reading tomorrow's headlines, today.

"My God, My God, why have You forsaken Me? Why are You so far from helping Me, and from the words of My groaning?" (Psalm 22:1)

Don't forget that the Torah was written in Hebrew, so this passage reads "Eloi, Eloi, lama sabachthani?" These words from the cross were meant to lead the audience to the purpose of His death. Jesus wanted them to know why He was dying. His words were not spoken because He believed God forsook Him, but because He believed the Jews were missing *why* He was there. He knew they would interpret His hanging on a tree as a curse for blasphemy, and though He was dying as a curse, it would be years (in the ministry of the Apostle Paul) before the Spirit would reveal that truth to man. He wanted to steer them, not toward God turning His back on Jesus, but toward *them* turning their backs on Jesus. Even in death Jesus was trying to save His audience!

Though Jesus is using this verse to direct the reader to the entire body of the 22nd Psalm, it must still be dealt with as a verse on its own. We closed the last chapter with a description of whom God was forsaking at Calvary, pointing firmly to Israel, so that He could direct His favor toward the entire earth. This is the cause for John the Baptist's shocking statement, "Behold! The Lamb of God who takes away the sin of the world!" (John 1:29) John is broadening the scope of Jesus' pending sacrifice to include the whole of the earth and not just Israel.

We should also note that it is David who writes this Psalm. The opening words of the song certainly speak volumes to us about the events of the future crucifixion, but they should also be viewed through the lens of the speaker, who no doubt felt that God had forsaken him on more than one occasion, and that God was not listening to his prayers. We know better (and I believe David did too), but let us not be quick to denigrate those who falter in their faith when they face persecution and loss.

Having identified the author, and at least some of his intent, we should also point out that this Psalm is written from the viewpoint of someone other than the author. David writes it as a prophecy, for the events happening to the subject had not happened to David, nor would they at a future time. The early church recognized this chapter as a description of events happening to Jesus in His death, but that revelation came years later. John quotes this chapter (John 19:24) and the author of Hebrews does the same (Hebrews 2:12).

The Highlights

I will not attempt to write a verse-by-verse commentary on Psalm 22, but I do want to point out some highlights that I think point clearly to the cross of Jesus Christ. Some are so obvious that the crowd could not have missed them. Others may require a bit more revelation. Again, these things come in stages, so whether or not everyone there understood them, we can't be sure, but we can know what Jesus was pointing to and why. I also do not assume that my personal conclusions are definitive. I am simply looking for Jesus through the text.

"O My God, I cry in the daytime, but You do not hear; and in the night season, and am not silent." (Psalm 22:2)

The book of Mark specifies that it was on the 3rd hour of the day when Jesus went onto the cross (Mark 15:25). This has Jesus being crucified at 9:00 in the morning. Eight verses later, Mark tells us that when the sixth hour arrived (noon), there was darkness over the whole land until the ninth hour (3 p.m.). At that time, Jesus cried out Psalm 22:1, drank a sponge full of sour wine, cried out again, "and breathed His last" (Mark 15:37). From these scriptural clues, we conclude that Jesus was alive on the cross for approximately six hours. Halfway through, at about the three hour mark, the sky turned black, and remained that way for nearly three hours, before Jesus gave up the ghost and died.

This progression of light to darkness and back to light again, coupled with several statements that Jesus made while on the cross, line up with the prophecy of Psalm 22:2. Jesus suffered and cried out in both the daytime and in the night season. His audience would have still been buzzing about the oddity of darkness settling onto midday. A look at verse 2 of the Psalm from which Jesus was quoting might have given them revelation as to what they had just witnessed.

"But You are holy, enthroned in the praises of Israel." (Psalm 22:3)

God does not cease to be holy, even if the previous accusations are true. His holiness is not an action or a response; it is His character. The conjunction "But," speaks of a rebuttal on the part of the author. Even if all of this proves accurate, God doesn't cease to be holy.

I wish that all of God's people felt comfortable and open with questioning the norms upon which they were raised and have learned in the church. Question everything! It is only when we ask tough questions that we come up with hard sought answers. Even if what we are asking sounds sacrilegious or blasphemous, fear not; God loves the inquisitive heart.

When Job was going through his infamous difficulties, having lost family, possessions, and finally, his health, he wrongly accuses God of being the one that "taketh away" (Job 1:21). Yet, the reader has spent the first chapter of Job behind the scenes, watching a confrontation between God and Satan, and has learned that it wasn't God that killed Job's family, destroyed his home and plagued his crops. In light of Job's response and attitude, don't you think God would be angry with Job? According to the text, God thinks differently than we do. "In all this Job did not sin nor charge God with wrong" (Job 1:22). Job got it wrong, but God knew his heart even better than Job did. In other words, God remains holy, even when we don't think He is, and He isn't even angry that we were thinking that way!

> *"Our fathers trusted in You; they trusted, and You delivered them. They cried to You, and were delivered; they trusted in You, and were not ashamed."* (Psalm 22:4, 5)

These verses express the dual nature of authorship. Both David and Jesus are speaking throughout the chapter, with these verses leaning more toward the human understanding. The basis of faith for God's people, prior to the cross, was that their fathers had made it through difficulty and hard times. If the fathers trusted and they were delivered, there must be a reason: so that the children could come into the world. The children then learned to trust God in the same manner, and they expected to never have reason to be ashamed.

> *"But I am a worm, and no man; a reproach of men, and despised by the people."* (Psalm 22:6)

This statement borrows from the book of Job, where Bildad the Shuhite questions how a man can be righteous before God. "How much less man, who is a maggot, and a son of man, who is a worm?" (Job 25:6) Jesus is identifying

Himself as a "son of man" by calling Himself a worm. Let it be noted that this scripture is speaking volumes about the intent of Christ at Calvary.

The "reproach of men, and despised by the people," lines up perfectly with Isaiah's prophecy that the tender plant would be "despised and rejected by men" (Isaiah 53:3). The "men" of both prophesies would not represent the whole of humanity, but rather a select few from Judaism, of whom Jesus came to deliver. One could no doubt find thousands of people who had been influenced positively by Jesus during His earthly ministry, but on the morning of His trial and crucifixion, the crowd that assembled at Pilate's Hall was blood-thirsty. They, along with the throng gathered at Calvary, would be the crowd that Jesus would address from the cross, and thus they would represent for all time "the people," doomed to such a lot as being those who "despised" the Savior of the world.

> "All those who see Me ridicule Me; they shoot out the lip, they shake the head, saying, 'He trusted in the LORD, let Him rescue Him; let Him deliver Him, since He delights in Him!'" (Psalm 22:7, 8)

Matthew records three distinct groups of people who deride and mock Jesus on the cross. First, the crowd in general, "And those who passed by blasphemed Him, wagging their heads..." (Matthew 27:39). Then, the chief priests also, "mocking with the scribes and elders..." (Matthew 27:41). Finally, even the robbers, "who were crucified with Him reviled Him with the same thing" (Matthew 27:44).

They "Rolled" Together

> "He trusted in the LORD, let Him rescue Him; let Him deliver Him, since He delights in Him!" (Psalm 22:7, 8)

There is mockery on two fronts with this statement made by the chief priests, scribes and elders. To see the intensity of their sarcasm, we need to go to the original Hebrew to see what the English fails to bring out in the first front.

The Hebrew word used here for "trusted" is different from the one used a few verses earlier in Verses 4 and 5. In those verses ("Our fathers trusted in You..."), the word "trusted" is the Hebrew word "batach," and it means "to trust, to have confidence, to be secure." This definition lines up pretty closely to how we would define the word in English as well.

However, in verse 8, when the mocking statement "He trusted in the LORD" is used, the Hebrew word for "trusted" is "galal" which translates "to roll, roll away, roll down or roll together." It is never translated as "trusted" in any of the other 17 times it appears in the Old Testament. In fact, the word is translated as some variant of "roll," 12 times. I will not make an assumption as to why the translators chose to use "trusted" in this particular translation, but I do wish to point out the proper translation of the word to show what those mocking Jesus might have been referencing.

Five of the first seven uses of "galal" in the Old Testament have to do with stones being rolled. Stones were always rolled by men as a collaborative effort, most of the time to offer water from a well. Jesus has presented Himself as the giver of "a fountain of water springing up into everlasting life," while sitting on Jacob's well (John 4:6, 14), and also as "living water" while watching the chief priest draw water in John 7. He also made His famous "Take (or roll) away the stone," statement in John 11:39. Those mocking Him could be referencing these acts.

More likely, the use of "galal" to mock Jesus is in regards to Jesus' statements of His unity with the Father. In a confrontation with a group of Jews that were persecuting Him, and looking to put Him to death, Jesus told them, "My Father has been working until now, and I have been working" (John 5:17). That did nothing but infuriate them, leading Jesus to qualify further.

> "Most assuredly, I say to you, the Son can do nothing of Himself, but what He sees the Father do; for whatever He does, the Son also does in like manner. For the Father loves the Son and shows Him all things that He Himself does; and He will show Him greater works than these, that you may marvel." (John 5:19, 20)

This passage shows Jesus' feelings about His own work, as inspired of the Father and in perfect unity with Him. He declares that whatever God does, He does "in like manner," and that He does it because His Father loves Him and prefers Him. These statements could contribute to the use of "galal," as one definition is "to roll together." By stating this, they are basically stating, "He thought He rolled with God? Then let God save Him!"

The second jab of sarcasm is found in the final phrase of Verse 8, "Let Him deliver Him, since He delights in Him!" The scribes and chief priests certainly did not think that Jesus was beloved of God or that God found delight in Him. This statement is a mockery of the rumor that they had heard of the moment at Jordan where the Spirit descended in the form of a dove and the crowd heard the voice from heaven state, "This is My beloved Son, in whom I am well pleased" (Matthew 3:17). I doubt that story went over well with the Jewish hierarchy, and they had probably spent most of Jesus' earthly ministry working to dispel its validity.

The Bulls of Bashan

"Many bulls have surrounded Me; strong bulls of Bashan have encircled Me. They gape at Me with their mouths, like a raging and roaring lion." (Psalm 22:12, 13)

Jesus uses two animals metaphorically, to describe the veracity of the assembled mob. The bull and the lion are both kings of their domain, and both are often used in conjunction with violence or dominance. Peter uses similar imagery in warning his readers of their common enemy, "because your adversary the devil walks about like a roaring lion, seeking whom he may devour" (1 Peter 5:8).

The second "bulls" in the Verse is italicized in the Authorized Translation (King James Version), because it does not appear in the original Hebrew text. Read without it, the verse still states that bulls have surrounded Him, but "strong of Bashan have encircled Me" could indicate a reference to something else.

The "strong of Bashan" would have been familiar to a student of the Torah. During Israel's wilderness experience, the Israelites sought permission to journey through the land of the Amorites and were denied access by their king, Sihon. Rather than simply deny Israel passage, Sihon gathered his armies together and fought against Israel. With God on their side, the Israelites prevailed with a crushing victory that basically left the whole of Ammon theirs for the taking.

Turning onward to continue their march, they were met by King Og of Bashan. The legend of this mighty man, no doubt, preceded him.

When Israel heard that Og was on the move, there must have been a general wave of fear and dread, for Moses specifically records the Lord's words to him. "Do not fear him, for I have delivered him and all his people and his land into your hand; you shall do to him as you did to Sihon king of the Amorites, who dwelt at Heshbon" (Deuteronomy 3:2).

Perhaps the fear was due to more than just the size of the army of Bashan, but to the size of King Og himself.

> *"For only Og king of Bashan remained of the remnant of the giants. Indeed his bedstead was an iron bedstead. (Is it not in Rabbah of the people of Ammon?) Nine cubits is its length and four cubits its width, according to the standard cubit."* (Deuteronomy 3:11)

Bashan had come to be associated with the giant Og, and this imagery should not be forgotten when we read Psalm 22. The giants of mockery, adversity, condemnation and persecution were howling at Jesus while He hung on the cross. The reproach Jesus underwent was a substitute for all of humanity. If the giant Goliath could hurl accusation and condemnation at David, and David could defeat him by pleading his covenant of protection, then the Son of David could face the giant of Bashan, a symbol of the last giant, and defeat him with the cutting of an even better covenant!

> *"For even Christ did not please Himself; but as it is written, 'The reproaches of those who reproached You fell on Me."* (Romans 15:3)

When shame and reproach is hurled at us, we can view Jesus as our substitute. He was attacked and ridiculed so we do not have to own the attacks and ridicule!

A Look at the Physical

The purpose of this chapter is not to give a medical rendering of what happened to Jesus on the cross, nor is it to give opinion as to the severity of the wounds He suffered. I save medical insight for the professionals, researchers, and theologians far smarter than myself. I want to see the spiritual behind the physical, while still maintaining our original purpose: to see through the scriptures what Jesus wanted the gathered throng at Calvary, to see.

Through the first thirteen verses of Psalm 22, the descriptions of the Suffering Savior have been primarily through verbal attacks. There have been no descriptions of His physical suffering. Anyone who might have taken up Jesus' challenge of consulting the 22nd Psalm to find out what was happening at Calvary would have had to use a bit of discernment to connect the subject of the Psalm with the suffering of Jesus. However, beginning with the 14th verse, the middle portion of this song will describe various physical ailments and actual scenarios, which would be undeniably prophetic of Jesus' crucifixion, to even the most stubborn reader.

> *"I am poured out like water, and all My bones are out of joint; My heart is like wax; it has melted within Me."* (Psalm 22:14)

The phrase "poured out," is the Hebrew word, "shaphak." The word is closely associated with the shedding of blood. In fact, its first usage in the Old Testament is found in Genesis, just after Noah and his family leave the ark.

> *"Whoever sheds man's blood, by man his blood shall be shed; for in the image of God He made man."* (Genesis 9:6)

Both the plural and the singular form of the word are modern translations of "shaphak." This sets a precedent, which is picked up at various times throughout the Old Testament. When Jesus declares, "I am poured out like water," He is referencing His shed blood, being poured out of His body, like water from a pitcher.

His phrase, "all My bones are out of joint," parallels well with another Messianic prophecy from Psalm 34:20, which John quotes in his gospel, "Not one of His bones shall be broken" (John 19:36). Though none of His bones were broken, the hanging of the crucifixion would have, no doubt, pulled his arms from their sockets, and perhaps the same could be said for other joints. The gruesome nature of the hanging would have been evident to all, and the pain of such would have shown on any victim's face and through his actions.

Blood and Water

"…My heart is like wax; it has melted within Me." (Psalm 22:14)

Again, I save the medical description of this for the experts. I want to find deeper meaning in the spiritual. Christ's heart melting like wax could speak of a deep sense of pain and loss that He felt for Israel in their rejection. He articulated that in Luke 13:34, while weeping over Jerusalem and His entire ministry was aimed at the lost sheep of the house of Israel. Their rejection of the long-awaited Messiah melted His heart.

The most physical explanation is found in the last moments before bodies were removed from the crosses at Calvary. The Jews asked Pilate to break the legs of the three crucified men, as this would remove their ability to hold themselves up on the cross, effectively suffocating them to death. This hastening of death was a necessity, as the next day was a high Sabbath, and the bodies needed to be off the cross.

> *"But when they came to Jesus and saw that He was already dead, they did not break His legs. But one of the soldiers pierced His side with a spear, and immediately blood and water came out."* (John 19:33, 34)

The description of the soldier piercing Jesus' side with a spear is found only in John's gospel. Perhaps the other writers left it out because it happened after Jesus was finished speaking, or because it was post-mortem. Whatever the reason for the absence of this story in all other Gospel accounts, John includes it because of the phenomenon of it (it was not common for the victim to have died so soon, so a spear-piercing was unusual), and so that in knowing, we might believe.

> *"And he who has seen has testified, and his testimony is true; and he knows that he is telling the truth, so that you may believe."* (John 19:35)

The same author was so impressed by this event (perhaps that is why he includes it?) that he eventually came to see it as the representation of the Godhead as well as the core of salvation.

"This is He who came by water and blood – Jesus Christ; not only by water, but by water and blood. And it is the Spirit who bears witness, because the Spirit is truth. For there are three that bear witness in heaven: the Father, the Word, and the Holy Spirit; and these three are one. And there are three that bear witness on earth: the Spirit, the water, and the blood; and these three agree as one." (1 John 5:6-8)

The three "that bear witness on earth," are a vital part of our understanding our own redemption. The Spirit lives in the believer because the blood of Jesus cleansed them from their sin, and water baptism identified them with the burial and resurrection of Christ. This is the role of "the three" in our salvation identification.

The three-fold Spirit, water, and blood, also play an important role in our day-to-day walk with Christ. All work in concert, thus creating perfect agreement. In this, they are "one." The Spirit convicts us of our right-standing with the Father (John 16:10), since we are reconciled to Him by the death of the Son (2 Corinthians 5:18; Romans 5:10). The blood makes this possible, as it is what justifies us in the sight of God (Romans 5:9), sparing us from His wrath. Just like the blood on the doorposts of the Israelite homes in Egypt, God has seen the blood, has identified that a "just" death has occurred, and has "passed over" us!

The water continues its role as well. Not only does it perform its symbolic work through water baptism, but it does its spiritual work through a daily spiritual "cleanse," of sorts. Jesus told His disciples, "You are already clean because of the word which I have spoken to you," (John 15:3). The "word" was all of the things that Jesus had ministered into their lives during their time together. His word cleansed them then, and it does the same now.

Paul told husbands to love their wives, "just as Christ also loved the church and gave Himself for her" (Ephesians 5:25). Having shown what Jesus *did* (gave Himself), he proceeds into the next verse to show what Jesus *will do*.

"That He might sanctify and cleanse her with the washing of water by the word, that He might present her to Himself a glorious church, not having spot or wrinkle or any such things, but that she should be holy and without blemish." (Ephesians 5:26, 27)

The cleansing of the church is performed by Jesus washing her over with water that is "by the word." The water keeps on cleansing through the words of Jesus, or we could say, through the "Word." In our text from 1 John 5, the apostle refers to "the Father, the Word, and the Holy Spirit," literally calling Jesus, "the Word." When Jesus speaks, His words cleanse us. He IS the Word!

Remember, Jesus told the disciples they were "already clean" because of the words He had spoken to them. This was to complete a thought from two chapters earlier, when Jesus went to His knees to wash the feet of His disciples. At first, Peter refused to allow the Lord to wash his feet, but then relented when Jesus said, "If I do not wash you, you have no part with Me" (John 13:8). Peter decides that if the washing of the feet is good, then the washing of the whole body is better. Keep in mind Jesus' statement, "already clean," when you consider the following:

"Jesus said to him, 'He who is bathed needs only to wash his feet, but is completely clean; and you are clean, but not all of you.' For He knew who would betray Him; therefore He said, 'You are not all clean.'" (John 13:10, 11)

Jesus cleansed His disciples with His words, and instructed them, through the illustrated sermon of foot-washing, that they should clean one another in similar manner. The whole spirit-man need not be washed off but once (salvation; 'washed in the blood'), but the feet, which trod through a world of filth and sin, need a daily cleansing. While the blood plays the important role of cleansing us from all sin, it is the daily cleansing of the water of His word that puts a blessed assurance in our hearts that we are His own.

The spear that pierced His side melted His heart like wax, and blood and water flowed forth from the wound. The mixture of the precious blood and water speak to the saint for all time. Out of the heart of our Savior came the blood of redemption and the water of washing. Both are from His heart, for both represent His truest passion and desire.

A Bride from His Side

The piercing of Christ's heart at the point of a Roman spear, also served a covenantal purpose that first surfaced in the Garden of Eden.

When God wished to make a helper for Adam, He pulled forth animals from the ground and marched them in front of His prized creation (Genesis 2:18, 19). When the animals proved less than suitable, God "caused a deep sleep to fall on Adam, and he slept; and He took one of his ribs, and closed up the flesh in its place" (Genesis 2:21). From the side of man, God brought forth woman, and joined the two together as husband and wife.

The Apostle Paul did a comparison between Adam and Jesus, calling one "first" and the other "last." The first Adam was a living being, while the last Adam was a life-giving spirit. The first was of the earth, made of dust; the second is the Lord from heaven (1 Corinthians 15:45, 46). This gives us precedent for comparing what the two "Adams" went through.

As far back as the book of Isaiah, God referred to Himself as a husband to Israel. To the same Corinthian church that he introduced the theme of "two Adams," Paul expressed a godly jealousy, "For I have betrothed you to one husband, that I may present you as a chaste virgin to Christ" (2 Corinthians 11:2). Also, to the church at Rome, Paul boldly pronounces that believers have become, "dead to the law through the body of Christ, that you may be married to another – to Him who was raised from the dead, that we should bear fruit to God" (Romans 7:4).

With the comparisons of Adam and Jesus fresh in your heart, consider that in Genesis, at "the beginning," and in a garden, God put Adam to sleep and pulled a bride out of his side. Then, at Calvary, the last Adam (Jesus) went to sleep and God pulled a bride out of His side, in the form of blood and water. This was a new beginning, birthed in a new garden, with an empty tomb. At Calvary, the sinner was cleansed, and the church was born!

With the flowing of the blood and the water coming from the birthplace of Adam's bride, we are now identified by that blood and water. We are not a typical religion, where we do good in order to achieve a future reward, or work to please God so He will be good to us and keep us alive. We have a relationship, forged in blood, and birthed through water. Like a child that has his parent's blood coursing through his veins, he entered the world through the water of natural birth. We are His forever, through the identifying marks of a blood and water birth. We are the bride, birthed from His side, protected beneath His wing, founded near His heart.

The Thirsty Savior

"My strength is dried up like a potsherd, and My tongue clings to My jaws; you have brought Me to the dust of death." (Psalm 22:15)

This reference to Jesus' tongue clinging to His jaws would not have been lost on those who happened to be close enough to the cross to witness two important events. Both events would involve sour wine, with one instance showing a refusal to drink on Christ's part, and the other showing a willingness to do the same. Why the change of heart?

Just as Jesus arrives at Golgotha, the soldiers were apparently moved with His exhaustion and decided to intervene. They had already ordered Simon of Cyrene to carry His cross to the peak of the hill, then they turn toward satiating His thirst before they nail Him to the wood.

"They gave Him sour wine mingled with gall to drink. But when He tasted it, He would not drink." (Matthew 27:34)

His refusal to drink was not because the wine was sour, as an event in His near future will prove. He knew what they were giving Him, but there was something about the way it tasted that caused Him to refuse to drink, though His body badly needed the hydration.

Gall - also known as myrrh - was a green herb, often used for medicinal purposes, that tended to numb or dull pain. Jesus refused the sour wine because it had been mixed with gall by the soldiers, who intended to provide Him some relief. I find it precious that my Jesus refused any pain-numbing agent at Calvary so that He could bear the full brunt of God's judgment on my behalf. He took no easy way out in paying for my indiscretions. Oh, what a Savior!

If the story of Jesus' thirst ended there, it would be quite remarkable. However, according to scripture, it would also be unfinished. When Jesus had suffered on the cross for many hours, His tongue was still clinging to His jaws:

> *"After this, Jesus, knowing that all things were now accomplished, that the Scripture might be fulfilled, said, 'I thirst!'"* (John 19:28)

Most center-column reference Bibles state that the scripture Jesus was fulfilling was our verse from Psalm 22, regarding His tongue clinging to His jaws. I won't disagree that there is a connection between the two, as His public pronouncement of thirst would have been remembered by His audience who took the time to read Psalm 22. They would have seen the 15th verse and it would have been a firm reminder of what truly occurred. With that said, I think Jesus was fulfilling more when He cried out.

> *"Now a vessel full of sour wine was sitting there; and they filled a sponge with sour wine, put it on hyssop, and put it to His mouth."* (John 19:29)

It's quite possible that the vessel sitting near the cross, full of soured wine, was the same vessel the soldiers drew from prior to the crucifixion. In the first instance, they mingled the wine with gall and Jesus rejected it. This time however, there is no mention of gall being mixed with the sour wine.

> *"So when Jesus had received the sour wine, He said, 'It is finished!' And bowing His head, He gave up His Spirit."* (John 19:30)

There can be no doubt, based upon the 30th verse, that Jesus drank the sour wine He was offered while on the cross. Hours earlier, He had rejected it due to the pain-reducing gall mixed in. Now, He requests it and accepts it, before crying out "It is finished!" There is plenty to be said at a later point about that powerful, final phrase of Jesus. At this time, I want to concentrate on why the drinking of sour wine would be the final act necessary for Jesus to accomplish before He could release His Spirit and die.

An Ancient Proverb

Just before Jeremiah introduces a passage regarding the New Covenant (which Jesus ushered in), God makes a statement regarding a long-standing mindset about the Old Covenant.

> *"In those days they shall say no more: 'The fathers have eaten sour grapes, and the children's teeth are set on edge.' But every one shall die for his own iniquity; every man who eats the sour grapes, his teeth shall be set on edge."* (Jeremiah 31:29, 30)

To the prophet Ezekiel, God brings up the old proverb again, with a new demand:

> *"The word of the LORD came to me again, saying, 'What do you mean when you use this proverb concerning the land of Israel, saying: 'The fathers have eaten sour grapes, and the children's teeth are set on edge'? As I live,' says the LORD GOD, 'you shall no longer use this proverb in Israel.'"* (Ezekiel 18:1-3)

The Jews had developed a little proverb to help explain a theological point. Their metaphor involved a man eating sour grapes, or drinking sour wine, and the stinging effect that such would have on his mouth was not felt by he who drank it, but rather by his son. The proverb was meant to show that if the father did something wrong, the sting of that error would be felt most harshly on his offspring. Israel held to this idea as a sort of "generational curse." We dealt with the breaking of the curse of the law by Christ on Calvary back in Chapter Three. We also dealt with the idea of a "firstborn curse." Let's see what else Jesus paid for!

The theological point that the sour grape proverb was helping to explain is found in the giving of the law to Moses on Mount Sinai. During God's giving of the Ten Commandments, He interjects a stern warning:

"For I, the LORD your God, am a jealous God, visiting the iniquity of the fathers upon the children to the third and fourth generations of those who hate Me." (Exodus 20:5)

The warning is clear: when a man sins, the judgment for that sin can be expected to carry down at least four generations. This meant that men were paying for the sins of their fathers for all of their lives. Any sickness could be the result of your father's sin. Bankruptcy, poverty, violence, rebellion: all of it was traceable to the failures of previous generations. This held a sense of dread and condemnation over all of Israel, as people knew they were paying for their family's failures, and they were creating more problems down the road for their own offspring with every sin.

God was ready for that old system of generational curses to come to an end. His preference was for a time when man would be responsible for his own life, rather than be held accountable for someone else's. When He robed Himself in human flesh in the form of Jesus, that time had come. In order to assure that no one would ever again be held accountable for the sins of another, Jesus jumped into the middle of that old parable and cried out, "I thirst," knowing full well that the sour wine was available at the foot of the cross. This time, without the mixture of gall, Jesus drank it, feeling the full sting of that soured wine against His own teeth. He drank the result of sour grapes (sour wine), so that our teeth would never be set on edge. He bore the brunt of the judgment, so we would never be judged! In taking the sour wine, His death was truly our own.

The Most Obvious Reference

I find the next verse in our progression through Psalm 22 to be the most obvious and telling reference to Christ on the cross that we have seen until this point. No one that accepted His challenge to find "My God, My God…" could have read this next verse without acknowledging that at the very least, the victim of Psalm 22 was dying on a cross.

"For dogs have surrounded Me; the congregation of the wicked has enclosed Me. They pierced My hands and My feet." (Psalm 22:16)

The historical record shows how crucifixion was performed (whether there were three nails or four is unimportant). Even without the historical record, we have the words of Jesus to Thomas, which confirms at least two of the three major wounds Jesus suffered at Calvary.

> "Then He said to Thomas, 'Reach your finger here, and look at My hands; and reach your hand here, and put it into My side. Do not be unbelieving, but believing.'" (John 20:27)

The more scripturally astute at the foot of the cross might have also remembered a prophecy from the book of Zechariah:

> "And one shall say unto him, What are these wounds in thine hands? Then he shall answer, Those with which I was wounded in the house of my friends." (Zechariah 13:6 KJV)

"Pierced"

There has been much disagreement regarding the Hebrew translation of "pierced," in Psalm 22:16. In some biblical translations it is made to sound more as a pinning down by outward forces, rather than as a piercing. To be fair, the English word actually translates from two Hebrew words in this passage. The first is "karah" which means "to dig or excavate." That could certainly deal with nail piercings in the hands and feet of Jesus, but it is the second word that has caused so much contention. The second is "ariy," the Hebrew word for "lion." It would thus read, "karah ariy," or "to dig lion."

The dogs that surrounded the cross were not literal animals, and thus the "lion" of the Hebrew translation shouldn't be considered literal either. Since one is metaphorical, it makes sense to assume as much from the other. The dogs were the congregation of the wicked that encircled Jesus and put Him on a cross. These were the same dogs that "pierce" His hands and His feet, or, the same dogs that dug into the hands and feet of the Lion. Revelation 5:5 describes Jesus as "the Lion of the tribe of Judah," so one doesn't have to take too far a leap to arrive at Jesus being the lion of the Psalm.

"I can count all My bones. They look and stare at Me." (Psalm 22:17)

The brutal pre-crucifixion beating that Jesus suffered at the hands of the Roman soldiers would account for this verse. With the flesh having been ripped away, the bones would be bare in many places, visible to all. This would be an image so grotesque that anyone would remember it vividly for the remainder of their days on earth.

The Garments of Jesus

"They divide My garments among them, and for My clothing they cast lots." (Psalm 22:18)

The Gospels of Matthew and John record that the soldiers responsible for crucifying Jesus tore His garment into four pieces, each taking a section of the robe as a souvenir. His outer garment, the tunic, was woven from the top down so that it was seamless. Much more valuable, this garment was considered too wonderful to tear, so the soldiers cast lots for it, meaning that they gambled for Christ's outer robe. This fulfilled the scripture that prophesied as much, yet more proof to those standing nearby that Christ's was no ordinary death.

This could be the most remarkable indicator of the authenticity of scripture and of prophecy. This group of Roman soldiers had no knowledge of the Torah, or of the prophecies regarding the Man on the cross. Their insistence on dividing the garments and then refusing to tear the tunic, but rather to cast lots for it, was a perfect fulfillment of scripture, and they had no idea what they were doing!

It also makes an interesting study to note that the same garment which the soldiers handled so freely, and without obvious repercussions, is the same one touched by the woman with the issue of blood. Having lived with this malady for years, she reached forth with faith and grabbed the garment by the edge, believing that it would be sufficient for her healing. She was correct, and her bleeding stopped. The soldiers handle the same garment, but display no such faith and receive nothing for their efforts, for the power of Christ was not in His garments, or His shoes, or any other such object. Similarly, there is no power to be found in touring the "Holy Land," or seeing His empty tomb. The power of Christ has always been accessible by faith, to those who will simply believe.

> "But You, O LORD, do not be far from Me; O My Strength, hasten to help Me!" (Psalm 22:19)

Until this point in the Psalm, Jesus only referred to His Father by the title "God." While on earth, Jesus is recorded as referring to Him as "Father," exclusively, until He quotes Psalm 22:1 from the cross, calling Him, "My God." The only other reference, by name, to God in this chapter came from the lips of the naysayers in verse 8, when they mockingly said, "He trusted in the LORD..." This word "LORD" holds special meaning.

When the "all-caps" version of "LORD" appears in scripture, it was translated as such to show the intent of the original Hebrew. In this case, it means Jehovah, which is a reference to Covenant Lord. When "Jehovah," or "LORD" is invoked, it is to bring out the covenant keeping quality of God's character. It is not to insinuate a different God exists, but rather that God has different qualities and characteristics.

When Jesus uses "LORD" in verse 19, it is to point the Father back to the purpose of the cross. We should not insinuate that God forgot, nor that Jesus thought His Father had forgotten. This is not the case at all. The Hebrew ideology was to point back to covenant through observances and ceremony so that the emphasis was placed upon the original intent. In Judaism, the Passover was observed to recognize the fulfillment of a covenant that God had made to Abraham in delivering His people out of bondage. Christian communion is a classic example of this, as we partake of the body and the blood of our Lord Jesus in order to remember the covenant that He cut with the Father at the cross, and to emphasize in ourselves all that He paid for.

We will learn more in future chapters about the covenant aspect of Calvary from the viewpoint of Heaven and from that of Jesus. In this, we will learn what Jesus paid for and what He provided with that payment.

The Declaration to His Brethren

*"I will declare Your name to My brethren; in the midst of the assembly
I will praise You."* (Psalm 22:22)

In the Epistle to the Hebrews, the author makes the argument that God was intent on bringing His glory out through "many sons," and that doing so would require the suffering of "the captain of their salvation" (Hebrews 2:10). This declares that God would sacrifice His "only begotten Son" in order to spiritually adopt an entire family of sons, eliminating any distance between Himself and His human family. It is this unity, the author argues, for which, "He is not ashamed to call them brethren" (Hebrews 2:11). Then, in Hebrews 2:12 he quotes our verse from Psalm 22:22. This gives insight into the thinking of the theologians of the first century. The writer of Hebrews has made another connection, linking the 22nd Psalm and its victim to our Savior at Calvary.

Paul viewed the Finished Work of Jesus in the same manner. He declared that all things work together for good to those who are within God's purpose, and that His purpose had to do with the development of a family.

*"For whom he foreknew, He also predestined to be conformed to the
image of His Son, that He might be the firstborn among many brethren."* (Romans 8:29)

I believe that this sheds more light on Christ's intent on calling us His brethren, as it speaks beyond a bloodline relation that He had with Jews, and more towards a spiritual connection that we have with Him by faith. This is confirmed by the idea that He is never recorded as having called His disciples His "brethren," during His earthly ministry, but when Mary Magdalene came to the empty tomb on Resurrection Morning, Jesus instructed her to "go to My brethren and say to them, 'I am ascending to My Father and your Father, and to My God and your God'" (John 20:17). Following the completion of His Finished Work of death and resurrection, Jesus called them His brethren and linked them under the same Father. Calvary now became the starting point of a greater family than national Israel. Jesus instituted a larger sense of adoption and belonging that went beyond familial heritage and delved into the realm of spiritual relationship.

"You who fear the LORD, praise Him! All you descendants of Jacob, glorify Him, and fear Him, all you offspring of Israel!" (Psalm 22:23)

This is a Jewish specific verse that pointed the Israelite to the death of Christ as a dual signpost: He died for them and His death increased the Jewish fear of the Lord, as there must be a pending judgment for their wholesale rejection of Him. This judgment was fulfilled less than a generation later, when the Roman armies leveled Jerusalem and destroyed both their temple and their religious system.

The Smoking Gun

If a key is needed to unlock the mystery behind, "My God, My God, why have You forsaken Me?" then we have finally found our way through the door. The argument has been made many times that God forsook Jesus at Calvary, and we opened this chapter stating that there is scriptural evidence to refute such an argument. The smoking gun verse, the one that describes BOTH, what God WAS doing and what God WAS NOT doing, comes next.

"For He has not despised nor abhorred the affliction of the afflicted; nor has He hidden His face from Him; but when He cried to Him, He heard." (Psalm 22:24)

The afflicted one from the Verse's first half is found to be Jesus in the Verse's middle portion. This means that the first part is not some blanket statement about God in non-specific terms, but is specifically aimed at the happenings of the cross. He did not despise what was happening to Jesus, nor did He abhor the affliction of His Son.

As we discussed in Chapter 2, it was men who killed Jesus on the cross, but it was God who saw all of our sins and our sicknesses in Jesus and then bruised Him. This appeasement of God's wrath against sin has ensured that He is pleased with us. This is why He did not despise or abhor the affliction of Jesus. Such affliction was necessary since God did not want to punish sins in the body of the sinner. It is not negligence on God's part; it is active participation in the necessary triumph of the cross!

"Nor has He hidden His face from Him," causes an obvious problem for proponents of the "God forsook Jesus at Calvary" argument. This verse makes it clear that God never hid His face from His Son on the cross. While it might make for a good sermon to say that God turned His back on His Son because He always turns away from sin, it doesn't hold water theologically. First, God wouldn't be viewing the cross as a sacrifice if He were to turn away from Jesus because Jesus was bearing all of our sins. The priest who killed the lamb in the tabernacle didn't turn away from the lamb during the sacrifice. He faced the lamb and finished the work, head on. God couldn't turn away at Calvary because only He was (and is) holy enough to face the failures of humanity and walk away unsullied. The second, and most obvious reason that the argument is weak theologically, is that the Psalm makes it clear that God, under no circumstances, would hide from His Son. This clears the confusion for me, making it obvious that Jesus was not being forsaken at Calvary, left to die alone and confused. God wasn't looking away or abandoning Him, for to look away would have been an act of cowardice on the part of the Father. Our sins demanded His full attention: anything less and the work goes unfinished.

I know the immediate reaction to the previous statements may be, "If God didn't turn His face from Jesus, then why did the sky go black? Wasn't this a response of the earth during the abandonment of the Son?" Later, in our title chapter, we will give a biblical explanation for the darkness that I think will be both revelatory and exciting. For now, let us continue down the road together, learning more about the fullness of His Finished Work.

A Promising Prophecy

"All the ends of the world shall remember and turn to the LORD, and all the families of the nations shall worship before You." (Psalm 22:27)

How glorious! The Finished Work of Jesus will eventually cause the whole earth to turn to the covenant keeping God. The cross ensures that the covenant they turn to will not be one of works and law, but one of everlasting promises. This will lead to all cultures and peoples knowing whom He is. We are seeing this even in this hour.

> *"For the kingdom is the LORD's, and He rules over the nations."*
> (Psalm 22:28)

No fear, believer. No matter what happens in your kingdom (wherever that might be), we have a King, who is sitting on His throne, in His Kingdom, and that Kingdom is not on some planet in another solar system, but it is "in your midst" (Luke 17:21). He will not be King *someday.* He is "King of kings and Lord of lords," *now!* (1 Timothy 6:14)

> *"All the prosperous of the earth shall eat and worship; all those who go down to the dust shall bow before Him, even he who cannot keep himself alive."* (Psalm 22:29)

The cross is the Great Equalizer. What politicians and governments have tried to accomplish in legislating equalities and opportunities, has already been paid for and accomplished through Christ's Finished Work. Both the prosperous and the poverty stricken find their solace in Him. Neither is more or less important at Calvary, for the cross delivers them equally: the prosperous, from leaning on his own wealth, wisdom and understanding and the poor, from allowing the chains of such to define and swallow him. Calvary never promised a car in every garage and money in every account, but it did promise to be the salvation and the life for all, whether one needs no help and support to live, or whether one "cannot keep himself alive."

> *"A posterity shall serve Him. It will be recounted of the Lord to the next generation."* (Psalm 22:30)

We are a part of the posterity that shall serve Him, as well as every generation that has done so since the cross. The word "next" in Verse 30 is italicized, thus we know the "generation" that has the message of the cross recounted, or retold, to them is not only the one generation following the crucifixion. Every generation since Calvary has heard the story, and it only gets sweeter with each retelling.

I find this to be so heart-warming. No matter what the situation brings, or how dark the world may appear, there will always be a generation serving Christ and telling others about Him! Don't be fooled by the naysayers who are saying things are only getting worse. They can't be *only* getting worse as long as there is "a posterity!"

He Has Finished

"They will come and declare His righteousness to a people who will be born, that He has done this." (Psalm 22:31)

When Jesus pointed the crowd at the cross to Psalm 22, He knew the ending to the song, and what a glorious promise it would be to those who grasped what He was accomplishing. This psalm ends with the promise that His righteousness would be declared to a people who were not even living at the time. This is another wonderful, two-fold promise.

First, the declaration will be regarding Christ's righteousness. This is the righteousness spoken of by Paul.

> *"But now the righteousness of God apart from the law is revealed, being witnessed by the Law and the Prophets, even the righteousness of God, through faith in Jesus Christ, to all and on all who believe. For there is no difference."* (Romans 3:21, 22)

Both the Law and the Prophets witnessed God's righteousness apart from the law. Jesus is that righteousness and He was witnessed by the Law (Moses) and the Prophets (Elijah) at Transfiguration. This righteousness is accessible, "through faith in Jesus Christ." By believing on Him, we are actually made into His righteousness (2 Corinthians 5:21).

The righteousness available to mankind prior to the cross was the righteousness of the law, found only in keeping the letter of the law. However, righteousness was impossible through that system, as Paul said. "Therefore by the deeds of the law no flesh will be justified in His sight, for by the law is the knowledge of sin" (Romans 3:20).

Second, the promise includes "a people who will be born." I claim this prophecy as happening in our midst, everyday! As long as there is someone "who will be born," there is a promise that the righteousness of Jesus will be declared. The wonderful message of God's amazing grace finds its foundation in the Finished Work of Christ, and that message has an audience in this, and every, generation.

The declaration of His righteousness is accompanied by the phrase, "that He has done this," and there is something in that final statement that is remarkable. It is important to notice that the final word, "this," is italicized, so the sentence should end after, "that He has done." The Hebrew word used for "done" is "asah" and it means "to be made or to be done." It parallels perfectly with Jesus' words on the cross, "It is finished," which John stated to be the final words of Christ on the cross (John 19:30). Again, consider that the audience at the cross had already been challenged to go to the Torah and read the Psalm that speaks of His violent death. The last phrase they would have read would have been the same as the last phrase they heard at the cross. "He has finished," would ring as loudly as "It is finished!" Jesus had taken them from the top of the Psalm, to the bottom, right before their very eyes.

The message of grace is the message of "It is finished!" We are declaring the work against sin and death to be finished. Jesus has won the victory, and there is no one left on the field. His work is not on hold, awaiting a future event in order to kick-start some cosmic clock back into action. He finished the work and declared as much. Now, we declare that same message. God give us the strength and courage to continue to do so, even to a generation of people, "who will be born."

Chapter 6

The Cross
As a Covenant

When we consider how many people were healed, restored and had general improvement in their lives due to the ministry of Jesus, it is hard to fathom that anyone would ever long to be anywhere but in His presence. But, as wonderful as His life was, and as open as He was to all that He encountered, not even Jesus had perfect retention among His followers. We are well aware of the disciple that betrayed Him, and the other that denied Him, but we may need reminded that these two were not the first of His followers to choose a different path. The Great Healer once said something so profound and offensive, that a large number of His disciples abandoned Him forever.

> *"From that time many of His disciples went back and walked with Him no more."* (John 6:66)

What did Jesus say or do that was so offensive? The context of this passage in John shows Jesus feeding the 5000, with the now famous "five barley loaves and two small fish." After this miracle, He walked on the water and then ministered to the early morning crowd on the other side of the sea. The trouble began within His own people (Jews), "because He said, 'I am the bread which came down from heaven'" (John 6:41).

It can be difficult for us, two thousand years removed from the event, and light-years away culturally, to understand why this statement was so offensive to the audience gathered around Jesus. Let's tackle the issue with a breakdown of what Jesus said, coupled with how they responded. With these, we can then learn why they felt the way they did.

> *"I am the living bread which came down from heaven. If anyone eats of this bread, he will live forever; and the bread that I shall give is My flesh, which I shall give for the life of the world." The Jews therefore quarreled among themselves, saying, 'How can this man give us His flesh to eat?"* (John 6:51, 52)

When Jesus called Himself, "living bread," He was showing a contrast to the bread their forefathers ate in the wilderness. That wilderness bread was called manna, and the Jews who ate it had been dead for centuries. Jesus stated that He was a different bread, not one that appears on the ground outside the tent every morning, but one that "came down from heaven." The bread is His "flesh," which He said He will give for the life of the world. This brought up the argument among the crowd that it was impossible for Him to give His flesh for them to eat. One can see both a primary and a secondary application in this argument.

Primarily, they remembered the miracle of the loaves and fishes which had occurred less than a day before. He had given them a meal to eat, but it had been borrowed from a little boy and multiplied to feed thousands. They don't see how it was possible for Him to have even more food to give them.

Secondly, the more spiritually astute were cautious about His statement regarding giving His flesh to eat, for it bordered on blasphemy in the Jewish religion. They partook of the flesh of a roasted lamb every year on Passover as a celebration of their covenant with God. This practice was instituted on the night they left Egyptian bondage, and it was repeated on the top of Mount Sinai, when seventy elders entered into a covenant of works and law by sharing a covenant meal with God (Exodus 24:11). To eat the flesh of *another* lamb could be construed as a breaking of their first covenant with God.

Keep in mind that the majority of people who were near Jesus, including those who had been cleansed and healed, were Jews, and that most of them DID NOT view Jesus as they viewed God. To them, He *might* be the Son of God, but certainly not on par with the God of Abraham. Due to this mentality, they were not prepared to enter into a relationship with Jesus that held the same elements as the communion of their Old Covenant.

> *"Then Jesus said to them, 'Most assuredly, I say to you, unless you eat the flesh of the Son of Man and drink His blood, you have no life in you. Whoever eats My flesh and drinks My blood has eternal life, and I will raise him up at the last day. For My flesh is food indeed, and My blood is drink indeed. He who eats My flesh and drinks My blood abides in Me, and I in him."* (John 6:53-56)

There can be little doubt at this point that Jesus claimed to be the giver of eternal life, and that life was accessible by consuming His flesh and drinking His blood. Those who thought in the natural were surely sickened at the cannibalistic tones of His language, while the spiritual among them were bothered at the covenantal implications He was giving. Next, He goes for the throat:

> *"As the living Father sent Me, and I live because of the Father, so he who feeds on Me will live because of Me. This is the bread which came down from heaven – not as your fathers ate the manna, and are dead. He who eats this bread will live forever."* (John 6:57, 58)

Jesus has now placed Himself on par with the Father, and thrown down the spiritual gauntlet by proclaiming that He is:

A. Sent from God and sustained by the life of God

B. The physical manifestation of the spiritual manna from the wilderness

C. From heaven

D. Greater than their forefathers, and can give life that the forefathers missed out on.

It doesn't take much insight to see why His own disciples called this "a hard saying" (John 6:60). Their statement prompted Jesus to say that it was the Spirit who gave life; "the flesh profits nothing. The words that I speak to you are spirit, and they are life" (John 6:63). It should have been very clear through this answer that Jesus was not about to cut off pieces of His flesh and drain His blood so that they could literally eat Him. He was inviting all to a spiritual feast in which they could participate in a covenant meal with Him.

Let it not be lost on the reader, for it was certainly not lost on the audience in that hour: Jesus was inviting mankind to enter into a covenant relationship with Him. He was offering to be an active participant with humanity in this covenant. To do so would require a severing of previous covenantal relationships in favor of a new one (New Covenant) with Him. He doesn't offer to explain the details of the covenant at this point, for as we will find later, this covenant will be loaded with promises and implications. He is simply showing them how to be a participant.

In the waning hours before journeying to the Garden of Gethsemane, and ultimately to the cross, Jesus partook of one final meal with His disciples. Their participation in this "Last Supper," would mark their revelation of one covenant being fulfilled in Christ, and a new covenant beginning.

> *"Then He said to them, 'With fervent desire I have desired to eat this Passover with you before I suffer; for I say to you, I will no longer eat of it until it is fulfilled in the kingdom of God.'"* (Luke 22:15, 16)

The Greek word for "desire," is translated elsewhere in the New Testament as "passion" or "lust." Perhaps the translators felt that such a translation here would seem sordid, but I, for one, wish they had shown the power of Jesus' "desire." He lusted with a great lust to eat that meal with them, for He was excited about being the fulfillment to the Passover. For centuries, Jews had consumed the Passover lamb and feared the awful judgment of God. Jesus was going to the cross as a new Lamb, and all who ate of that Lamb could live in hope and not fear. The judgment was complete, and the kingdom had arrived!

Consequently, the kingdom of God has obviously come, as the 18th Verse says it must, since we realize we are no longer under the rule of Passover observance. If we are NOT in the kingdom of God, in at least a partial fulfillment, then according to Jesus' own statement of Verse 16, the Passover ceremony is not fulfilled, and the greater Lamb has not yet died. His death on the cross fulfilled that Jewish requirement, as He has become the Passover Lamb for the world.

The Guarantee

The book of Hebrews details the framework of the New Covenant in comparison with the Old Covenant like no other. It highlights the difference in a natural priesthood like Aaron's and a supernatural priesthood like Melchizedek's, bringing light onto the everlasting priesthood of Jesus Christ. Written to the Hebrew people, it is specifically aimed at Jews who have come into the salvation by faith offered by Jesus and who are being tempted to go back under the old forms of Judaism.

The first several chapters are a pronouncement of the superiority of Jesus to all others, i.e. angels, Moses, Aaron. After asserting Jesus' prominence over the Levitical priesthood, the author states that "Jesus has become a surety of a better covenant" (Hebrews 7:22). The word "surety," means "guarantee," telling us that in order to see the promises of a better covenant, one must see them in Jesus, for He is the guarantee that they will come to pass.

> *"But now He has obtained a more excellent ministry, inasmuch as He is also Mediator of a better covenant, which was established on better promises."* (Hebrews 8:6)

In His resurrected form, Jesus now functions in the role of Mediator between God and man to ensure covenant promises. The cross, among its many applications, was a cutting of covenant, providing man with benefits that are accessible only through relationship with Jesus Christ. As the sacrificial Lamb, Jesus ushered in an entirely new system of spiritual government. In spite of the fact that some lobby for a return to an Old Testament-like system of theocratic government, there can be no denying, according to scripture, that the covenant that particular system was functioning under was in need of replacement.

> *"In that He says, 'A new covenant,' He has made the first obsolete. Now what is becoming obsolete and growing old is ready to vanish away."* (Hebrews 8:13)

The Old Covenant, which was "becoming obsolete" and "growing old" at the time of the writing to Hebrews, has since vanished away, just as the scripture said it would. This is supported by the opening context of the book, as it begins by telling the reader that God has spoken to the fathers by the prophets and "has in these last days spoken to us by His Son" (Hebrews 1:2). The "last days" could not be speaking of the end of the world as *we* know it, since the book was penned nearly 2000 years ago. Those "last days" would be speaking to the title audience, the Hebrew people, warning them that their very system of religion was on its last leg.

Another connection of Hebrews between the end of one covenant and the beginning of another can be made further into the book. As the author has already established the "last days" as the time in which they were living, and the Old Covenant as being "ready to vanish away," he goes on to show exactly why he thinks that the world of works religion is about finished, and why Jesus is unlike all other earthly priests:

> "He then would have had to suffer often since the foundation of the world; but now, once at the end of the ages, He has appeared to put away sin by the sacrifice of Himself." (Hebrews 9:26)

The "end of the ages" that Jesus appeared at in His first incarnation was obviously not the end of all ages or you wouldn't be here reading this book. His appearance marked a sort of "beginning of the end," as it regarded the Old Covenant and all of the Mosaic economy. Once He put away sin "by the sacrifice of Himself" (Hebrews 9:26), there was no more need for the Old Covenant system of animal sacrifices, which could never take away sins in the first place (Hebrews 10:4).

The Fault with the First Covenant

> "For if that first covenant had been faultless, then no place would have been sought for a second." (Hebrews 8:7)

When the text refers to a "first covenant," it cannot be making a reference to the first covenant ever cut between God and man. That would stretch back to Adam, with another covenant following with Noah, and then another with Abraham. The number of covenants would start to pile up, and an argument could be made regarding which "number" we are on now. For purposes of simplicity, the New Testament authors broke the whole covenant system down to the contrast of an old and a new or a first and a second. Paul used the two covenants concept in his letter to Galatia, using Hagar and Sarah as allegorical examples of both covenants (though neither covenant was anywhere to be found during either of their lifetimes).

> *"For these are the two covenants: the one from Mount Sinai which gives birth to bondage, which is Hagar — for this Hagar is Mount Sinai in Arabia, and corresponds to Jerusalem which now is, and is in bondage with her children — but the Jerusalem above is free which is the mother of us all."* (Galatians 4:24-26)

With Paul giving sanction to the idea of two covenants, as opposed to numerous ones, and then identifying the first one as from Mount Sinai, we are safe in viewing the first covenant as the one given to Moses on the mountain. This makes the first covenant the Mosaic Covenant, which includes all of the Jewish law and the Ten Commandments.

The author of Hebrews plainly states that there was a fault to be found with the "first covenant." If there had been no fault, then there would have been no reason to bother replacing it. Taken out of context, this scripture could be used to imply that God had designed a faulty covenant, one that was less than perfect and needed replaced. This would have enormous ramifications regarding God's creative ability, and it would be diametrically opposed to Paul's statement regarding the law:

> *"Therefore the law is holy, and the commandment holy and just and good."* (Romans 7:12)

The "therefore" that leads this verse, harkens back to something previous. Paul was speaking of how sin took opportunity by the commandment and produced in him all manner of evil desires (Romans 7:8). He wasn't saying that the law produced sin, but that sin found its empowerment through the law. To the church at Corinth he made a similar comment:

> *"The sting of death is sin, and the strength of sin is the law."* (1 Corinthians 15:56)

Sin actually found its strength in the presence of the law. Paul stated that he was fine until, "the commandment came, sin revived and I died" (Romans 7:9). These statements lead to the "therefore" of Verse 12, in which he declares that in spite of the error worked in him due to sin, there was nothing actually wrong with the law itself. The law is holy and the commandments found within the law are just and they are good.

This leads us back to the fault found with the first covenant. Hebrews states that there was a fault, while Paul says the law is holy, just and good. Which one is correct? What if I were to say, "Both"?

Let's go back to the verse from Hebrews and investigate the context. Beginning with the latter verses of the fourth chapter, the book of Hebrews brings emphasis onto the priesthood of Jesus. To show how He is our High Priest, the author laid out the qualifications for high priesthood and then matched those up with Jesus. Outside of a digression of thought at the end of Chapter Five and into Chapter Six, the author stuck primarily to this theme on through the Seventh and then into the Eighth chapters. He begins to sum it up at the outset of our chapter.

> "Now this is the main point of the things we are saying: We have such a High Priest, who is seated at the right hand of the throne of the Majesty in the heavens." (Hebrews 8:1)

The "main point" of the previous chapters was to emphasize the office of High Priest that Jesus currently holds for the believer. This was a necessary transition for the Hebrew reader to make as they were being weaned off of the earthly priesthood of Judaism. The reader is then challenged by the fact that Jesus has "obtained a more excellent ministry," as contrasted with the ministry of the priests of Israel. That brings us to the verse in question, followed by its necessary contextual partner:

> "For if that first covenant had been faultless, then no place would have been sought for a second. Because finding fault with _them_, He says: 'Behold, the days are coming, says the LORD, when I will make a new covenant with the house of Israel and with the house of Judah.'" (Hebrews 8:7, 8)

I put emphasis on the important word "them" from Verse 8. The fault that God found was not with the covenant itself, but with someone involved in the covenant. The reason we spent a couple of paragraphs dealing with the context of our passage in Hebrews was to give you an idea about who "them" might be. If the priesthood was the main subject of the book until this point, then the fault with the first covenant would be found in that priesthood.

As Goes the Priesthood...

The fault with the Old Covenant lay in its functionary arm. The priesthood is the subject of much of the book of Hebrews because it was at fault in its role of serving the people who were under that Old Covenant. I'm not insinuating that the men involved were all wicked or hypocritical, but by their very nature as representative liaisons of the people to God, they were woefully unqualified to represent them as anything other than fallen men, prone to failure, sickness and death. "For the law appoints as high priests men who have weakness..." (Hebrews 7:28).

A priest represented man to God, while the prophet represented God to man. Jesus is both prophet and priest in that He was the living image of His Father (prophet) while now serving as mediator on behalf of man (priest). When the priest was a mere man, he was forced to offer sacrifices for sins for himself, because, as a man, he had the failures of a man. Jesus was superior to that form of priesthood in every way, "...But the word of the oath, which came after the law, appoints the Son who has been perfected forever" (Hebrews 7:28).

> "For every high priest taken from among men is appointed for men in things pertaining to God, that he may offer both gifts and sacrifices for sins." (Hebrews 5:1)

Originally, the word "pertaining" is not found in Greek, so the verse could read "appointed for men in things to God," and it would work perfectly as a definition of the Jewish priesthood. They were appointed for men in things toward God.

The priesthood of Israel was made up of the tribe of Levi, and was supported financially by the tithes in Israel, "in return for the work which they perform" (Numbers 18:21). This financial supplement was considered their paycheck of sorts, since Levites were to have no inheritance of land like all the other tribes of Israel. In exchange for this lack of inheritance, the priesthood was paid out of the tithes, their bread was taken from leftover tabernacle showbread, and their meat was gathered from the sacrifices that came off the altar. In other words, their lives were provided for by the entire sacrificial system.

Since the high priest was in charge of the annual, national sacrifice (Day of Atonement), he was the representative for the people towards God. When God looked at the priest, He was looking at the ceremonial head of Israel. The focus of heaven was isolated on that priest, and God gave warning of as much.

> *"Hereafter the children of Israel shall not come near the tabernacle of meeting, lest they bear sin and die. But the Levites shall perform the work of the tabernacle of meeting, and they shall bear their iniquity; it shall be a statute forever, throughout your generations, that among the children of Israel they shall have no inheritance."*
> (Numbers 18:22, 23)

Israel had no right to come near the tabernacle, for their sin was too great. God appointed the high priest to come near the tabernacle on their behalf, and thus, the priesthood, "shall bear their iniquity." This put an enormous responsibility on the priesthood to come before the Lord as a faultless man.

Due to a wicked priesthood, Israel found itself in trouble on more than one occasion. The priesthood of Eli, as told in the first three chapters of 1 Samuel, is an example of what happened to the nation when the family of priests lived dishonorably. The Philistines conquered Israel and stole the Ark of the Covenant, all of which could have, and should have been avoided. This was a problem; a fault; an issue. The glaring fault was to be found in that first covenant, in which an entire nation was judged based upon a flawed priesthood.

The good news is that if the first priesthood was the problem under the Old Covenant, and our Jesus is now our High Priest, mediating a better covenant, built upon better promises, then we are in very good hands! As goes our priest, so we go. If Jesus is deemed worthy, then those covered under His Covenant are deemed worthy. Again, this is not due to our works, but due to His Finished Work. The cross now clearly becomes the beginning of a new priesthood.

A Necessary Change of the Law

I want to address one more issue that has surfaced in this portion of the study before we move on to a deeper look at the covenant cut at Calvary. The New Covenant helps put to rest old mindsets and paradigms that are bound within religious tradition. Some of those traditions are cultural or generational, while others are crossovers from other religions, (such as Jewish traditions finding their way into the Christian church). While it may seem holy to have such observances, no mixture of old and new ever turns out good. Let's seek the purity of a new paradigm, founded on the principles of grace and favor.

A few paragraphs ago, we brought out the fact that the priesthood was provided for by the tithes of the people. The author of Hebrews addresses this issue and then injects Jesus into the equation.

> "And indeed those who are of the sons of Levi, who receive the priesthood, have a commandment to receive tithes from the people according to the law, that is, from their brethren, though they have come from the loins of Abraham." (Hebrews 7:5)

Notice that the receiving of tithes was a "commandment" or a law for the priesthood. This commandment was due to the fact that these mortal men had no earthly inheritance, and thus their inheritance was the tithe. What if there was a priesthood made up of immortality? Would they need a mortal possession? If the priesthood of mortal men was working properly, why replace it?

> "Therefore, if perfection were through the Levitical priesthood (for under it the people received the law), what further need was there that another priest should rise according to the order of Melchizedek, and not be called according to the order of Aaron?" (Hebrews 7:11)

Jesus is the priest "according to the order of Melchizedek," which is a priestly order without a beginning or an end. He is compared to the priest that met

Abraham in Genesis 14, and is prophesied of in Psalm 110:4. The system of the priesthood underwent a change, from multiple priests, to one priest.

> *"Also there were many priests, because they were prevented by death from continuing. But He, because He continues forever, has an unchangeable priesthood."* (Hebrews 7:23, 24)

If the old system of tithing and supporting the priesthood through the food and bread left over from sacrifice was due to the fact that the priesthood needed a mortal inheritance, wouldn't there be a change in these elements if a graduation occurred from a priesthood of the mortal, to a priesthood of the immortal? Or, to make it more plain, "If there is a new form of priest, shouldn't there be a change in everything else?"

> *"For the priesthood being changed, of necessity there is also a change of the law."* (Hebrews 7:12)

To which law is the author referring? Contextually, it appears to be those laws concerning the priesthood. The commandment to tithe in Verse 5 would qualify, since there is no need to support a natural priesthood in light of our supernatural priest. The law received by the people in Verse 11 falls within the context as well. This "law" references everything under the Levitical priesthood, which would pertain to the tithe, the sacrificial system and all items in the tabernacle. Verse 16 mentions the "law of a fleshly commandment," speaking even more about the difference in laws governing a fleshly priesthood versus the priesthood of Jesus which is "according to the power of an endless life" (Hebrews 7:16).

The Tithe

The concept of the tithe is decidedly Jewish, and was commanded under the law to support a natural priesthood. In Christianity, without a natural priesthood, we are under no such command. Paul's teachings on giving in 2 Corinthians chapters 8 and 9 do not contain one reference to the tithe, an odd fact indeed if tithing was considered standard fare for the early church. These chapters actually bear out teaching that runs *counter* to the concept of the tithe, which was a compulsory (mandatory) giving of 10% of one's income. Paul even speaks *against* such giving.

> *"So let each one give as he purposes in his heart, not grudgingly or of necessity; for God loves a cheerful giver."* (2 Corinthians 9:7)

Keeping the starting point of the New Covenant at the cross, where the sacrificial death of the Lamb instituted an entirely new system, one can also contextualize the statements of Jesus. His comments to the Pharisees about tithing have been used to put people back under the tithe, but remember *when* Jesus said this:

> *"But woe to you Pharisees! For you tithe mint and rue and all manner of herbs, and pass by justice and the love of God. These you ought to have done, without leaving the others undone."* (Luke 11:42)

Speaking to Jewish leaders, *under the law,* Jesus states that they should not leave out the giving of their tithes. Again, put this in perspective regarding timing (pre-Calvary; pre-New Covenant).

Finally, the argument is made that things like the tithe should be excluded from any statements concerning fulfilled law, because it pre-dates the giving of the law. This argument concludes that if something was instituted prior to the law, and it was given sanction by God, then it should logically continue after the law was fulfilled through the Finished Work. Based upon this logic, one should be sure and hold fast to this line of thinking in every area in which the rule applies. Admittedly, the tithe appeared prior to the law (Abraham paid tithes, as did Jacob), and is then instituted as a command under the law (to support the priesthood, which we covered), and thus, for argument's sake, should apply after fulfillment of the law. To be fair, let us keep that rule universal.

Animal Sacrifice

Animal sacrifice appeared before the law (every principal character in Genesis offers animal sacrifice; the law doesn't appear until Exodus 20), it is a staple of the Mosaic law (nearly every offering in the tabernacle contains animal parts), and thus it should continue after the law is fulfilled. Every church, by this rule, should have an altar where members sacrifice animals (by the way, an altar was never a wooden bench where you knelt and cried; it was an elevated place of execution). I hope you see the faultiness of such an argument. This would be a blatant return to Judaism, a slap in the face of the Finished Work of the true Lamb, and a revival of an old, archaic system. Since our sins are remitted, Hebrews says, "there is no longer an offering for sin" (Hebrews 10:18).

Obviously, the Christian church feels no need to return to the system of animal sacrifices, nor should we. We know we already have the ultimate sacrifice in our Jesus. Revelation shows us a glimpse into the heavenly realm, and into the midst of the throne, where there "stood a Lamb as though it had been slain" (Revelation 5:6). We recognize that Lamb as our Jesus, ever representing a slain sacrifice, on behalf of our sins, "and not for ours only but also for the whole world" (1 John 2:2).

The cross was the death of a Lamb, and it simultaneously put to death the old sacrificial system. For what the old system could only perform as a shadow, Jesus became the substance. The purpose of that shadow was an attempt to make those who were offering sacrifices, perfect. However, in this, the shadow failed.

> *"For the law, having a shadow of the good things to come, and not the very image of the things, can never with these same sacrifices, which they offer continually year by year, make those who approach perfect. For then would they not have ceased to be offered? For the worshipers, once purified, would have no more consciousness of sins. But in those sacrifices there is a reminder of sins every year."* (Hebrews 10:1-3)

If the sacrificial system was working in its attempt to make people perfect, wouldn't sacrifices have ceased to be offered? Once the worshipper was purified, he would have "no more consciousness of sins." Notice that the perfection mentioned in this passage does not insinuate that the worshipper would never sin again, but that he should have no more consciousness of sin. The sacrificial system failed in its attempt to take away man's sin consciousness.

When ministries try to make their adherents MORE sin conscious, under the guise that such consciousness will lead them away from sin, they are showing a misunderstanding of the purpose of the law. The sacrificial system only reminded the worshipper of his sins and thus he fell beneath the weight of that consciousness. The perfection achieved under a new sacrifice (Jesus) is not necessarily that the New Covenant believer never commits sin again, but that we are free from the burden of sin consciousness. When we are released from that burden, we are no longer a slave to sin, and true liberty comes from this new consciousness, or, "Savior consciousness."

Circumcision

Circumcision is another example of a principle that pre-dates the law (Abraham was told to circumcise his children as a sign of the covenant that he had with God), and then it was a command under the law (all Jewish boys were circumcised at 8-days old, and all men who converted to Judaism were not considered Israelites until they were circumcised). By the reasoning laid out previously, this practice should continue on now, even though the law is fulfilled. However, this argument runs into another snag, for we find that the Apostle Paul held strong beliefs against this practice continuing, even though it was both a right and a passage both before and during the law.

> "Indeed I, Paul, say to you that if you become circumcised, Christ will profit you nothing. And I testify again to every man who becomes circumcised that he is a debtor to keep the whole law…For in Christ Jesus neither circumcision nor uncircumcision avails anything, but faith working through love." (Galatians 5:2, 3, 6)

The prevailing argument in the early church, between those ministering righteousness by faith, independent from works, and those adhering to at least a partial return to the Mosaic Law for believers to maintain their righteousness, was the issue of circumcision. Paul preached that to add circumcision to your salvation was to return to the law for your righteousness. If you do this, you may as well forget Christ, for He "profits you nothing," and that to do so would be a "fall from grace" (Galatians 5:4). Paul simply chose the prevailing issue of his day to illustrate that what was only a shadow, had been replaced. Circumcision was no longer necessary, because a new cutting had taken place at Calvary.

"For he is not a Jew who is one outwardly, nor is circumcision that which is outward in the flesh; but he is a Jew who is one inwardly; and circumcision is that of the heart, in the Spirit, not in the letter; whose praise is not from men but from God." (Romans 2:28, 29)

The act of circumcision was given by God as a sign of the covenant He had made with Abraham. When seed passed through the sign of covenant, conception occurred beneath that same covenant. This assured the Israelites that their lineage came into the world beneath the covenant of protection that God had given Abraham. The practice was carried over into the law, and came to be understood as an identifier of Judaism.

When circumcision is performed for medical reasons or as a preference by parents for purposes other than religion, one should not read such conclusions into it. We are speaking from the standpoint of a religious practice, by which one derives some sense of righteousness. Of this, the Apostle Paul was adamantly against.

Cursed With a Curse

The changing of the priesthood signified a necessary change of the law. With Jesus as our new high priest, so many observances that were once considered absolutes had become absolutely unnecessary. Animal sacrifice was no longer needed, for our sacrifice was once for all (Hebrews 10:10). Circumcision for righteousness was both unnecessary and damaging (Galatians 5:2). The tithe, once established to fund the priesthood of Israel, is now without purpose, as there is no priesthood to fund. To tithe because one feels that it is the road to riches is to place greater emphasis on the shadow than the substance. Jesus was rich, "yet for your sakes He became poor, that you through His poverty might become rich" (2 Corinthians 8:9).

Interestingly, when one starts to view the cross as a Finished Work by which the law is fulfilled and true freedom is established, scriptures from the Old Covenant are brought up to explain this freedom away. The final book of the Old Testament has been used in such a role for many years.

"'Will a man rob God? Yet you have robbed Me! But you say, 'In what way have we robbed you?' In tithes and offerings. You are cursed with

a curse, for you have robbed Me, even this whole nation. Bring all the
tithes into the storehouse, that there may be food in My house, and
try Me now in this,' says the LORD of hosts, 'If I will not open for
you the windows of heaven and pour out for you such blessing that
there will not be room enough to receive it.'" (Malachi 3:8-10)

People don't quote Old Testament to try and put you back under animal sacrifice. Instead, they say that Jesus is the Lamb that was slain and no other sacrifice can help. They do not quote the law to convince you to circumcise your baby
boy. Instead, they tell you that Jesus was cut off from the living so a cutting could
occur in your heart, in which you are identified by a spiritual circumcision. But
when it comes to the tithe, Malachi gets quoted from pulpits every week, with the
threat of a financial curse and a drought of blessings. How is it that Jesus fulfilled
some, but not all? He did fulfill all! Look at three things.

First, Jesus was made to be a curse so that you could be free from any and all
curses of the law (See Galatians 3:13, 14). We covered this material in detail in
Chapter Three. Why would you allow yourself to be put under any curse, knowing
that Jesus has paid for all of them on your behalf?

Second, Malachi 3:8-10 is written to national Israel. Verse 9 says that the
whole nation had robbed God. This was not an individual warning, it was a corporate one.

Finally, the instruction of the Malachi warning was to bring all the tithes
"into the storehouse, that there may be food in My house." The storehouse was
where the tithes of the people went so that the priesthood could draw from it and
live. Notice that the purpose of the storehouse, within the context, is so that there
may be food in the house of God. This "house" of God, in the Old Testament,
was the tabernacle or the temple. Under the New Covenant, you are the temple
of the Holy Spirit, and there is no physical house of God (1 Corinthians 6:19).

One final thought on the tithe regards Hebrews 7:8, which states, "Here mortal men receive tithes, but there he receives them, of whom it is witnessed that he
lives." This verse is often interpreted to mean that when you tithe you testify of
the resurrection of Jesus. Such an interpretation even leads ministers of grace to
preach the tithe in order to show forth the life of Christ. However, this interpretation is taking the verse out of its context, and is another sneaky way of easing

works back into the beautiful privilege of grace giving. The act of tithing under the law was the funding of a Levitical priesthood, but those tithes were really going past Levi all the way to the one who has an endless priesthood, Melchizedek. It is not a verse condoning the practice in order to make Jesus appear alive, it is simply a passage explaining to Jews that there was always a greater priesthood than the Levitical, so the idea that Jesus is of a greater priesthood should not be considered sacrilegious to their sensibilities.

The Message says it perfectly:

> "Or look at it this way: We pay our tithes to priests who die, but Abraham paid tithes to a priest who, the Scripture says, "lives." Ultimately you could even say that since Levi descended from Abraham, who paid tithes to Melchizedek, when we pay tithes to the priestly tribe of Levi they end up with Melchizedek." (Hebrews 7:8-10 MSG)

Please note that the author says "when we pay tithes to the priestly tribe of Levi." He is referring to his Jewish readers (remember the book is written to Hebrews), who pay tithes to the tribe of Levi. You are not a Jewish reader and you do not pay tithes to the priestly tribe of Levi.

I realize it took several pages to investigate this area of the tithe, which incorporated several other Old Testament ideologies. I did this to shed light on some often overlooked areas under the New Covenant, and to put more glory on the place where all glory belongs: the Finished Work of our lovely Jesus. Let me make it clear that I am not advocating that believers stop giving into the work of God; I am simply encouraging them to be free from the obligation of doing so. Don't read the Bible, go to church, pray, witness, or give because you feel obligated to do so. This robs the joy and beauty of these things, all of which should be enjoyed as sons instead of performed as servants.

"I disregarded them..."

We have established that "them," whom God found fault with under the Old Covenant, was the priesthood and its flawed system. Take that thought one verse farther with the author.

"Because finding fault with them, He says: 'Behold, the days are coming, says the LORD, when I will make a new covenant with the house of Israel and with the house of Judah – not according to the covenant that I made with their fathers in the day when I took them by the hand to lead them out of the land of Egypt; because they did not continue in My covenant, and I disregarded them, says the LORD." (Hebrews 8:8, 9)

The speaker is the LORD, Jehovah, "Covenant God." He states that a new covenant is necessary with the house of Israel and the house of Judah, but that it will not be according to the covenant that He made with the generation that came out of Egypt. This is the Mosaic generation, which received the law on Mount Sinai. The reason for that Old Covenant being abolished is because He found fault, as we have explained. A new covenant is needed, "because they did not continue in My covenant," speaks of the failure of Israel to keep their end of the bargain, but the next line gives us something telling about the heart of God. "And I disregarded them, says the LORD."

The phrase, "I disregarded them," is a statement of neglect in Greek. God neglected His own people due to the fact that they "did not continue in My covenant." Can we resolve this thought with the fact that God never leaves us, or forsakes us? How can these two concepts be compatible? Realizing that God is an everlasting keeper of covenant, how could He establish a New Covenant through His Son?

The common answer to the previous question is, "God didn't break covenant, Israel did." The problem with that argument is that part of the covenant that God had with Israel was that He would not only bless them when they were obedient and good, but He would curse them when they were not. There is no end in sight for such a bargain. Israel broke their end of the covenant, which was to do everything that God had required of them, on more than one occasion. Israel breaking their end of the deal did not cause the covenant to be annulled, it simply required God to keep His end of the deal, which in the event of their failure was to punish and judge them. Can you see that Israel sinning did not constitute them breaking covenant? Their sin required God to *keep* His part of the covenant!

This erroneous idea that the Old Covenant was broken by sin makes no sense. If the covenant had stated that if Israel failed then God was free from any obligation toward them, then yes, sin would have broken the covenant. In reality, the Old Covenant should go on forever, as there is no room for it to end. God should have just kept on cursing them for as long as they were sinning.

In light of this information, we must strive to find the answers to a few important questions. If the New Covenant was made with the house of Israel and Judah, how are we involved, seeing as we are not all Jewish by blood? If that covenant was with Israel and Judah, then why was Jesus involved, as He is but one man among many Jews? Also, and I think this next one is one of the most important questions we can ask in regards to understanding the transition from one covenant to the next: If the Old Covenant rewarded good behavior and punished disobedience, how could it ever have been disregarded, according to Hebrews 8:9? Or, more plainly put, "How could God ever justify ending the Old Covenant?" The answer may surprise you, but it could also liberate you from a mentality of works, forever.

Chapter 7

Can God Break Covenant?

My own personal observation, shaped by a lifetime spent in the church, has persuaded me to believe that a large percentage of Christians suffer from a confusion that comes as a result of mixing the covenants. The New Covenant is embraced, by and large, for its simplicity of salvation, in which grace is both abundant and amazing for the repentant sinner. After conversion, the principles and focus of the Old Covenant are used in increasing measure in order to teach these new converts how to live. It is as if we have concluded that what makes the better covenant so much better is that we do not have to kill sheep in order to be "saved," while all other Old Covenant demands should still hold true. This confusion is damaging and binding, but it is not new.

We are not far removed, in our mentality, from the early adherents of Christianity, who had come out of the religion of Judaism. Many of those early saints felt guilty and condemned about abandoning Moses, and slowly but surely, they began to incorporate more and more principles of the Old Covenant into the simplicity of the New.

Paul was concerned about this simplicity being lost when he spoke of his fear in a letter to the church at Corinth:

> "But I fear, lest somehow, as the serpent deceived Eve by his craftiness, so your minds may be corrupted from the simplicity that is in Christ." (2 Corinthians 11:3)

The simplicity of Christ is simple faith: He died for you, and by identifying with Him in His death, you are raised in the same power of the Spirit into a new life in Christ Jesus. We may be excluding some deeper theological implications, but it is basically a simple doctrine. The serpent deceived Eve into eating from the forbidden tree for an increase in knowledge, and after Adam tasted the fruit, mankind was enslaved to a lifetime of works righteousness. Christ died on another tree, providing access back into the paradise lost by Adam's failure and ensuring perpetual righteousness through the Finished Work of the cross. Paul's concern for his church was that they would go back to that previous life of works, rather than to resting in the simplicity of Christ having finished the work. In short, Paul was concerned that Christians would return to the principles of Judaism.

Perhaps our obsession with the Old Covenant has less to do with a lack of faith in the New Covenant and its provisional promises, and more to do with the fact that Jesus lived the Old Covenant to perfection. If He lived the Law to perfection, and we are to strive to be more like Jesus, then naturally, it would appear that the highest standard of living would be the keeping of the Mosaic Law. In fact, many of us were taught that since we have Jesus living inside us, we now have the power to keep the law.

I will save the argument of whether or not our mandate as Christians is to be like Jesus ("…as He is, so are we in this world" – 1 John 4:17), and concentrate on the fact that Jesus did indeed fulfill the Mosaic Law. It would be difficult to find anyone to argue with that fact, as Jesus said as much about His purpose (Matthew 5:17). With that established, let's concentrate more on when He fulfilled the law. Did He fulfill it at the cross? We know He finished the work of redemption there, but is that the place where the Law of Moses was completely fulfilled?

I propose that if the fulfillment of the law came with Jesus' death on the cross, then it was a bit too late! The only thing that would qualify Jesus as the sacrifice for humanity is if He had fulfilled the legal requirements of the Mosaic Law *prior* to His crucifixion. His claim of "It is finished," would mark the end of the sacrificial requirement and the long standing war against sin, but fulfilling the law would have to have been done by His *works,* as the law was a part of the Old Covenant, built upon man's works in response to God's holy demands.

It is finished... Twice?

The first instance of Jesus finishing the work is found in a lengthy prayer He prays just before going to the cross. While the bulk of the prayer is in support of His disciples and all future believers (you and me included), the opening verses are a direct plea to the Father from the Son, regarding His own life and ministry.

"I have glorified You on the earth. I have finished the work which You have given Me to do." (John 17:4)

By Christ's own admission, He had "finished the work," even before He went to the cross. This is the first of two "finished" works. The second came at the end of the crucifixion saga, when Jesus declared "It is finished!" These two could be lumped into one, but that might also be robbing each instance of its individual importance.

Christ's declaration of "It is finished," from the cross speaks primarily to His offering Himself as a sacrifice. "It is finished," would denote an end to the sacrificial offering that Christ was performing, and would prelude "giving up His spirit" (John 19:30). While this definition is primary, I believe we are safe in seeing some other implications to Jesus' finishing the work.

The finished work of the John 17 prayer points to the life and ministry of Jesus in keeping the Father's will and fulfilling the Law. The finished work of the John 19 declaration speaks of the end of Calvary as a sacrifice and to other things as well, such as the long-standing war against the sin of the world. The prophecy in the Garden of Eden that declared the bruising of the Seed of the woman would mark a head-blow to the serpent Satan (Genesis 3:15), and it was finally fulfilled. Having paid for the sin of the world, Jesus finished the work in bridging the gap between fallen humanity and God. Reconciliation was complete (2 Corinthians 5:18, 19).

To uncover another layer beneath the Calvary declaration of "It is finished," we need to find one more unfulfilled portion of scripture within the Old Testament. Just as we detailed in Chapter 5 regarding Jesus' drinking the sour wine in order to fulfill an Old Testament promise, His statement about the finished work was fulfilling another promise as well. Again, consider that Jesus fulfilled the law with His life, and He declared as much in John 17:4. At Calvary, He knew He was finishing even more, with the most overlooked aspect concerning the actual Old Covenant itself.

Can God Break Covenant?

New Covenant preaching has often included the following statement, "God cannot break covenant." We say this, knowing that it helps explain the various judgmental aspects found in the Old Testament (under the Old Covenant) and it also gives solace to New Covenant people who are resting beneath a better covenant built upon better promises. My question however, is whether or not the statement is biblically accurate.

Let us dig into the Old Testament to unearth a prophetic scripture that could go a long way toward shaking our previous held ideas about covenant. Without context (we will get to that in detail in a moment), know that the speaker in the following verse is God, speaking to the prophet about a coming event:

> "And I took my staff, Beauty, and cut it in two, that I might break the covenant which I had made with all the peoples." (Zechariah 11:10)

It seems pretty clear that God uses the breaking of a staff as an illustrated sermon for how He will break the covenant that He made with His people. Again, we have established almost no context, but this verse raises the issue of God breaking covenant, an event which most of us would say, with little hesitation, is not possible.

The chief rebuttal to any argument regarding God breaking covenant comes almost universally because it is the most clear-cut, definitive scripture that seemingly solves the problem. It is found in the songbook of Israel, where again, God is the speaker.

> "My covenant I will not break, nor alter the word that has gone out of My lips." (Psalm 89:34)

Pretty cut and dry, right? God is the speaker in this passage, and He makes it clear that He will not break His covenant, nor will He say one thing and then change His mind. It appears, on the surface, that this is the end of the story. However, we cannot simply discount one scripture in favor of another, which might better serve our theology or our purpose. Can we reconcile the following thoughts?

- God states that He will not break covenant (Psalm 89:34).
- God states that He will break His covenant (Zechariah 11:10).

This apparent contradiction of terms and statements desperately needs some context! The passage from Zechariah holds wonderful truths that are best uncovered in light of the finished work, so let us begin with the scripture from the Psalmist that states that God will not break His covenant.

We should closely examine every verse of the chapter to do it justice, but I will leave that investigation to you during your own study. For purposes of finding where Verse 34 fits contextually, let's begin in Verse 20 and pick up the central character.

> "I have found My servant David; with My holy oil I have anointed him, with whom My hand shall be established; also My arm shall strengthen him." (Psalm 89:20, 21)

Obviously, the main character of the passage is David, whom we know to be the anointed king of Israel, chosen by God. God tells us that David has been anointed, is guided by the hand of God and is strengthened by His arm. From here, the verses give God's promises toward David, which include David outwitting his enemies (Verse 22); God being faithful and merciful to him (Verse 24); David dominating the seas and rivers (Verse 25); God considering David His firstborn and the highest among kings (Verse 27).

> "His seed also I will make to endure forever, and his throne as the days of heaven." (Psalm 89:29)

God promises to promote the seed of David on the earth forever and to honor his throne by establishing it "as the days of heaven," a statement which speaks of perpetuity. This promise was not fulfilled in the natural realm, as David's throne was cut off due to the failures of Israel and Judah, but in Christ, the new Son of David, the kingship and the throne continue on until this day.

In all of these verses, God is establishing a set of covenant standards. He now begins to specify what can be expected by subsequent generations following David. Remember, these are the framework statements of a covenant.

> *"If his sons forsake My law and do not walk in My judgments, if they break My statutes and do not keep My commandments, then I will punish their transgression with the rod, and their iniquity with stripes."* (Psalm 89:30-32)

Note the terms of punishment attached to David's sons in the event that they break God's law. Now watch, as God gives a promise on top of those guarantees:

> *"Nevertheless My lovingkindness I will not utterly take from him, nor allow My faithfulness to fail."* (Psalm 89:33)

God is promising to judge David's sons if they fail to obey Him, but He is also quick to point out that in spite of that discipline, He will not remove His kindness from them entirely. He will also be faithful to them, even when they are not faithful to Him. This leads into Verse 34, in which we learn that God will not break covenant. With this context, let us go past our key verse and see how God concludes the thought.

> *"Once I have sworn by My holiness; I will not lie to David: his seed shall endure forever, and his throne as the sun before Me; it shall be established forever like the moon, even like the faithful witness in the sky."* (Psalm 89:35-37)

From the statements made about David prior to Verse 34, and the follow-up statements about God's promises to David that come after Verse 34, we can conclude that the covenant God says that He will not break was a specific covenant. That 34th Verse speaks of the covenant that God cut with David, in which He promises to make his seed endure forever and his throne as the days of heaven. The 35th Verse says that God "will not lie to David." These verses cannot be used to speak arbitrarily about just any covenant. It should be obvious that the covenant that God cannot break is the one established with King David.

David understood his covenant with God to be unique and everlasting, as he asserted on his deathbed:

> *"Although my house is not so with God, yet He has made with me an everlasting covenant, ordered in all things and secure." (2 Samuel 23:5)*

He is not speaking of the Mosaic covenant of works here, for he admits that his house is not in order. Under the Mosaic covenant, one could expect to be rewarded when they did right and punished when they did wrong. In this prayer, David acknowledges that though his house is out of order, God has a specific covenant with him that is "everlasting" and that in it, all things are "ordered… and secure."

Further Confirmation

To solidify the case that the covenant God promises not to break in Psalm 89:34 is indeed His covenant with David, we find further confirmation in Jeremiah's writing.

> *"Thus says the LORD: 'If you can break My covenant with the day and My covenant with the night, so that there will not be day and night in their season, then My covenant may also be broken with David My servant, so that he shall not have a son to reign on his throne, and with the Levites, the priests, My ministers.'" (Jeremiah 33:20, 21)*

God offers a challenge: if you can stop the natural progression of day into night, then you can break God's covenant with David. Again, note that when speaking of the covenant that cannot be broken, God is speaking about His specific covenant with David.

An Everlasting Covenant

I hope it has been made clear that there is a distinct covenant being referred to in Psalm 89:34. The preceding segment has simply tried to establish that it is improper for one to use this Psalm as "proof" that God cannot break covenant. However, I *am not* trying to instill a lack of confidence in the everlasting qualities of the New Covenant. God Himself chose to establish an everlasting covenant with Israel that was based on the one He had with Abraham before them, and which He still upholds with His church, the seed of Abraham, to this day.

> *"For thus says the Lord GOD: 'I will deal with you as you have done, who despised the oath by breaking the covenant.'"* (Ezekiel 16:59)

Any discussion about God breaking covenant would not be complete without showing that Israel broke their end of the covenant *first*. God's response is to deal with them as they have dealt with Him.

> *"Nevertheless I will remember My covenant with you in the days of your youth, and I will establish an everlasting covenant with you."* (Ezekiel 16:60)

The "days of your youth," to which God is referring, could not be a time in which they functioned beneath a different covenant than they did as adults, nor does it mean that God dealt with them by covenant when they were young and then abandoned that covenant when they were old. Speaking to Israel collectively, as His child, His reference to the days of their youth would have been in regards to their earliest days as a people. More specifically, it involved the covenant that God made with Abraham, the patriarch of Israel. God is stating that with them having broken the Mosaic Covenant by totally abandoning Him for strange gods, He chooses to return to the covenant that He had made with Abraham. This covenant will someday (at Calvary), "provide you an atonement for all you have done" (Ezekiel 16:63).

Let's walk through the events one more time before we dig into God's breaking of covenant. Please note that this timeline is not exhaustive; it simply highlights what occurred:

- God calls Abraham out of his homeland and establishes an everlasting covenant with him, promising to multiply his seed and establish a people (Israel) through him.

- God delivers Israel from Egyptian bondage and enters into a covenant of works with them.

- God establishes a natural priesthood within Israel by which He judges and blesses them.

- God enters into an everlasting covenant with David, guaranteeing that his throne will last forever.

- Israel breaks covenant with God by rejecting Him, and God reciprocates and returns back to the Abrahamic covenant.

- Jesus Christ lives as God-in-flesh, fulfills the demands of the Law, becomes a heavenly priest replacing the earthly priesthood, and is the rightful King of kings, fulfilling God's promise to David.

- Christ's death and resurrection opens the door for the entire world (not just Israel) to enter into the everlasting covenant of Abraham, accessible by faith in Jesus Christ.

We have covered some of the above points in more detail than others, and we will attempt to remedy this before our journey together concludes. Now, let's turn fully to the topic of our chapter.

A Flock Marked for Slaughter

The conditions found in Zechariah for God to break covenant are very clear. The passage also speaks prophetically, revealing both how and when the breaking would occur. A contextual look at Zechariah 11, coupled with a connection to the Gospel account of Christ's crucifixion, will provide us with our answer. Let's begin in Verse 4 and work our way into the controversial 10th Verse.

> *"Thus says the LORD my God, 'Feed the flock for slaughter, whose owners slaughter them and feel no guilt; those who sell them say, 'Blessed be the LORD, for I am rich'; and their shepherds do not pity them.'"* (Zechariah 11:4, 5)

Hebrew syntax does not indicate that God wants a flock fed so that they can be slaughtered, or as we might refer to it as "fattened for the kill." Rather, another translation captures the essence: "Shepherd the flock marked for slaughter. Their buyers slaughter them and go unpunished. Those who sell them say, 'Praise the LORD, I am rich!' Their own shepherds do not spare them" (Zechariah 11:4, 5, NIV).

This prophecy speaks to a specific generation that was marked for slaughter, underneath "owners." As the context will bear out, we are looking at a prophecy of the time of Christ on earth in His first advent, when Israel was under the ownership of the Roman Empire. Rome could slaughter Israel wholesale and "feel no guilt" (Verse 5).

The Jewish rulers in Palestine, during the time of Christ, were in a habit of merchandising the people and the synagogue. Jesus confronted this attitude when He cleared the temple of the moneychangers, a group of people who were dishonest in their money exchange rates and who made it nearly impossible for the common man to afford passage into the rites of redemption. The Pharisees held rule even over the spiritual peace of the Jewish people, threatening to excommunicate them from the synagogue, and thus heaven, if they as much as offended the Pharisees' sensibilities (see the parents of the man born blind in John 5). The prophecy identifies them through the phrase, "those who sell them."

> *"'For I will no longer pity the inhabitants of the land,' says the LORD. 'But indeed I will give everyone into his neighbor's hand and into the hand of his king. They shall attack the land, and I will not deliver them from their hand.'"* (Zechariah 11:6)

God was obviously so fed up with the actions of Israel that He had no pity left for them. He promised to give them over to their neighbors, a prophecy fulfilled by the fact that Israel was living interspersed with Romans and peoples of all nations and tongues. He also declared that He would give them "into the hand of his king." Israel should have been exempt from such a prophecy during the time of Christ, for they had no king of their own. Herod was the political king over the region of Judea, but he held no spiritual kingship for Israel as a nation. Unfortunately, the attitude of the Jewish leaders during the arrest and trial of Jesus began to provide New Testament context for this entire prophecy.

"Now it was the Preparation Day of the Passover, and about the sixth hour. And he said to the Jews, 'Behold your King!' But they cried out, 'Away with Him, away with Him! Crucify Him!' Pilate said to them, 'Shall I crucify your King?' The chief priests answered, 'We have no king but Caesar!'" (John 19:14-15)

Did you catch the blatant blasphemy? The chief priests, those men appointed by God to represent the people to their King, declared that they had no king but Caesar. This is no misstatement or misunderstanding. They were fully aware of the ancient prophecy concerning kingship in Israel.

"The scepter shall not depart from Judah, nor a lawgiver from between his feet, until Shiloh comes; and to Him shall be the obedience of the people." (Genesis 49:10)

The scepter was a symbol of kingship and the prophecy declared that Shiloh (peace) would come and the people would be obedient to Him, as people are always subject to their king. Jesus was from the tribe of Judah and had declared peace everywhere He went. The chief priests were perfectly aware of this, and yet they denied Him as king and claimed Caesar, a self-proclaimed god-ruler, to be their king. The prophecy of Zechariah had found a home.

A Blinded Israel

There has been much debate as to whether or not Israel even could have accepted Jesus as their Messiah. This argument is based primarily on a statement in the gospel of John in which the Prophet Isaiah is being quoted:

"Therefore they could not believe, because Isaiah said again: 'He has blinded their eyes and hardened their hearts, lest they should see with their eyes, lest they should understand with their hearts and turn, so that I should heal them.'" (John 12:39-40)

John stated that they "could not believe," because "He has blinded their eyes and hardened their hearts." This would indicate that Israel was incapable of accepting Jesus as Messiah because God had made it impossible for them to do so. If that be the case, then how can He possibly judge them for rejecting someone that He wouldn't allow them to accept?

Paul followed this line of thinking in Romans 11:7 when he declared that Israel was "blinded," and in Verse 8, where God had given them, "a spirit of stupor." These passages were a source of great concern for me for quite some time, as I couldn't reconcile how God could blind Israel and then judge them for their blindness.

Thank God Paul considered himself a sufficient minister of the New Covenant! His proclamation as such in 2 Corinthians 3:6 was the lead-in to a passage on Israel's infatuation with the Mosaic Covenant. Paul called the Ten Commandments "the ministry of death" and "the ministry of condemnation" (3:7, 9). He admitted that it had glory, but that the glory on the Old Covenant was "passing away," and the remaining covenant was "much more glorious" (3:11).

Regarding Israel's inability to see the glories of a New Covenant, Paul gives us the fulfillment of the argument. Rather than painting God as working against Israel, ensuring their rejection of the Messiah, Paul shows that the advent of the law did just as much.

> *"But their minds were blinded. For until this day the same veil remains unlifted in the reading of the Old Testament, because the veil is taken away in Christ. But even to this day, when Moses is read, a veil lies on their heart. Nevertheless when one turns to the Lord, the veil is taken away."* (2 Corinthians 3:14-16)

The Mosaic Law had blinded the minds of Israel, making it impossible for them to see the beauty of the New Covenant, and the loveliness of Jesus. It has taught me that if we wish to make God appear unloving and unkind, and to take the shine off of Jesus, we should reinstitute a standard of laws and morals by which man feels righteous or unrighteous. The unheralded side-effect of that action would be a lack of faith in the Lord Jesus – precisely what happened to Israel.

Beauty and Bonds

"So I fed the flock for slaughter, in particular the poor of the flock. I took for myself two staffs: the one I called Beauty, and the other I called Bonds; and I fed the flock." (Zechariah 11:7)

The language here represents the Messiah, but was being spoken through Zechariah. Most likely, he literally performed the actions that he was speaking, but wrote them as directed by God. Thus, you are reading Zechariah, but you are seeing the actions of Jesus. This is well illustrated through the phrase "in particular the poor of the flock," as the poor were a constant concern of our Savior.

When Jesus was anointed with the Spirit at the Jordan River, His first mandate was "to preach the gospel to the poor" (Luke 4:18). When a young man wanted a works-based salvation, Jesus prompted him to sell all he had and give it to the poor, showing a high concern for those in poverty. He commended the giving spirit of the poor widow in Mark 12 whom He said gave more than the rest, for she gave from her poverty. In Luke 14, He encouraged the wealthy to throw wide their doors for the poor, the crippled, the lame and the blind. The principles of the Kingdom of God, of which Jesus was a conduit, are all aimed at helping those who cannot help themselves.

The prophecy now turns to an object lesson, with two staffs involved and named. One is called "Beauty" and the other, "Bonds." The Hebrew rendering of these are closer to "Grace" and "Unity." Their role in the story seems to emphasize the equipment of a shepherd and to serve as objects to break, in order to illustrate a breaking in the spirit realm. "Beauty" is "cut in two" in Verse 10 as a symbol of the breaking of covenant between God and His people. "Bonds" is broken in Verse 14, illustrating the breaking up of "the brotherhood between Judah and Israel." Notice the order in which they are broken: "Beauty" first and then "Bonds." The Mosaic covenant is broken first and then the further fracturing of the tribes of Israel and Judah ensues.

The Three Shepherds

"I dismissed the three shepherds in one month. My soul loathed them, and their soul also abhorred me." (Zechariah 11:8)

As we have seen, this entire prophecy is set sometime within the life of the Messiah. This is evidenced by the fact that Israel is under the power of the Roman Empire, with worthless shepherds that rob and fleece people for profit and who have identified themselves as under the kingship of Caesar. Now, a specific prophecy of three shepherds, or leaders, being removed in one month is spoken as if the reader should know who they are.

Theologians are divided in their interpretations of Verse 8. I tend to disagree with those that name these as three individuals, as there is a mutual dislike between the three shepherds and the Messiah, according to the last sentence of Verse 8. My dismissal of this opinion is due to the fact that I cannot wrap my mind around Jesus loathing people. Due to the nature of the prophecy until this point, in which the shepherds have sold the people and have no pity on the populace, I lean toward the idea that these three shepherds represent three *offices* of leadership within Judaism. Any office that stood in the way of humanity experiencing the manifestation of God would have brought out a loathing in Jesus, and for this cause, I adhere to this opinion. Furthermore, this thought seems to align itself well with the tone of the author who is writing a prophetic letter to an entirely Jewish audience. His matter-of-fact tone regarding three shepherds leads me to believe that the average reader would have had an automatic understanding of whom, or what, these shepherds were.

Some might point at scribes, Pharisees, and Saducees as the three offices, but I find the correlation even better to see the three shepherds as being offices that are descriptions of our Lord Jesus: *prophet, priest,* and *king.* More than three individuals, these three "shepherds" had been ruling over Israel for centuries, and in the cutting off of the Mosaic Covenant, they all met their demise. Jesus has been, is now, and forever will be, all three in one personality. He is the Prophet spoken of by Moses (Deuteronomy 18:18), the Priest promised by God (Hebrews 5:9, 10), and the King of kings (1 Timothy 6:15).

116 BETWEEN THE PIECES

The time span in which the three shepherds are "dismissed" or more properly translated, are "cut off," is one month. Proper exegesis of scripture would identify this as a fixed period of time, but not necessarily limited to one month. A comparison of a similar usage of time periods in prophecy would be found in Hosea 5:7, where a judgment is said to take place as "a New Moon shall devour them and their heritage." This is not a specific amount of time, but it falls within a timeframe.

Another example of this sort of literature being metaphorical is found in Revelation, regarding the Tree of Life in the New Jerusalem.

> *"In the middle of its street, and on either side of the river, was the tree of life, which bore twelve fruits, each tree yielding its fruit every month. The leaves of the tree were for the healing of the nations."* (Revelation 22:2)

Every month yielded a different fruit. It is possible that the imagery is meant to indicate that each month is a different period of life, full of its own individual beauties. This could be the reason there is a correlation between 12 fruits and 12 months. In any case, we can be assured that it is representative of something greater than a different flavor every 30 days.

> *"Then I said, 'I will not feed you. Let what is dying die, and what is perishing perish. Let those that are left eat each other's flesh.'"* (Zechariah 11:9)

So complete was God's abandonment of His rebellious people that He withheld feeding them. Jesus was the last hope for diet change in Israel, as He offered Himself as the bread of life. When they refused Him, they were refusing Heaven's best offer, and all that was left was to perish (thus Jesus' famous statement in John 3:16). The last sentence, "Let those that are left eat each other's flesh," was hauntingly fulfilled during the Roman invasion of Jerusalem in AD 70, when the isolated and starving inhabitants trapped within the city's walls were forced to cannibalism in order to survive.

God's Offer for Israel's Exit

Since we have covered Verse 10 at least in part, it is necessary to group the next few verses together in order to see the full picture of what was really happening when God had Zechariah break "Beauty," as a symbol of His breaking covenant with Israel. Read the text carefully and watch for the offer that God makes to Israel in order to buy Him out of the covenant, which by their actions, they badly want out of.

> "And I took my staff, Beauty, and cut it in two, that I might break the covenant which I had made with all the peoples. So it was broken on that day. Thus the poor of the flock, who were watching me, knew that it was the word of the LORD. Then I said to them, 'If it is agreeable to you, give me my wages; and if not, refrain.' So they weighed out for my wages thirty pieces of silver." (Zechariah 11:10-12)

When God breaks His staff as a sign of His covenant, He offers Israel the opportunity to buy Him out of His end of that covenant. If they wish to, He prompts them to "give me my wages." This marks the moment that God, frustrated with Israel's frequent breakings of the covenant, shows Israel an exit strategy. They can not only buy God out of the covenant, but they can set the price as His "wages." Whatever price they set would be viewed as the value they put on all that God had done for them through the Mosaic covenant. Before we deal with that value, let's properly illustrate what was happening in this prophecy by using more modern terminology.

If you want to buy a home, but you do not have the money to simply buy it outright, you can go to a bank, or other financial institution, to acquire the necessary funds. If you are credit-worthy, the bank will most likely enter into a contractual agreement with you, in which they provide you with the funds necessary to purchase the home from the seller. In addition to the money the bank is loaning you, they also permit you to live in the home and call it your own. The condition for this contract is that you must make timely, agreed upon payments to the bank until you have paid them in full for the loan, plus a specified amount of interest for their trouble.

Now, let's assume that at some point, several years into the agreement, you run into hard times financially and are having a difficult time making your monthly payments. The bank starts calling you daily, wanting their money, and the mailbox is full of collection notices and warnings of foreclosure. You are trying to catch up but you find yourself continually behind on payments and underwater on your mortgage. That 30-year note you signed at the beginning of the contract now seems like a mountain you simply cannot cross over. You love your home, but the inability to maintain it has you thinking of moving and living elsewhere, free from the stress of keeping up.

The options for exiting the contract are rather limited. One of these is to simply stop sending in payments, and eventually, the bank warnings and threats will end in foreclosure, and the bank will claim what they paid for all those years ago. The money you repaid them is lost to you, and the home you occupied is gone as well. The only "positive" is that you are out of the contract; but you are also out of the house!

The other option is to pay the bank in full for the remainder of the balance owed. This would release you from the contractual obligation of sending in a monthly payment. Of course, if this were a feasible option, you wouldn't be in dire straits in the first place, as you would not be behind on your payments, and you would not be living under the stress of possibly losing your home.

Let's insert another implausible, fictitious option into the story. Imagine that one day the banker comes to you with a proposition. He reminds you of the contract you signed, and the large amount of money you were loaned so you could purchase your lovely home. He states the bank has upheld its end of the bargain and has always expected to either receive payment in full, or to take back the house, but they are exhausted, and quite frankly, tired of dealing with you. They want out of the contract just as much as you do, and are willing to drop all litigation and future collection procedures for a lump sum payment totaling far less than you actually owe. While this is good news, you quickly interject you don't even have enough money to catch up your lapsed payments, much less come up with a lump sum for the home, even if that sum is far below what you actually owe. But here is where the story becomes even more unbelievable. The banker states they are so desperate to get out of the contract with you, since you obviously don't want to do business with them, that they are willing to take whatever you offer, no matter how small or insulting it might be.

I told you the illustration was implausible and fictitious! No bank would do this, for they could just foreclose on the home and kick you out and begin trying to recover their money through a future sale of the property, but that last option better illustrates what took place between God and Israel.

At Sinai, Israel entered into a covenant with God. God promised to provide them with protection and blessings, to fight their battles for them and to promote them tirelessly. In exchange, Israel paid for this protection with their undying obedience and allegiance to God. They agreed not to serve strange gods, nor bow down to idols, and they agreed to put God first in both their private lives and their national celebrations. If they failed in any of these things, God was *not* released from the covenant, but instead, He would reciprocate their insolence and disobedience with curses, famine, exile, and even death. In other words, if Israel did good things, God would respond with goodness, but if Israel did poorly, the covenant continued on with negative returns. Either way, they were in this covenant for keeps.

Having tired of Israel's repeated sins and transgressions, God saw that Israel blatantly wanted nothing to do with Him. Rather than continue on in the same manner in which they had gone for centuries, God decided to let them "keep the house" so to speak. They could have their identity, their temples, their religion, and their heritage, but He wanted nothing more to do with the obligation of blessing and cursing them. In order to break the covenant, He requested one, final, lump sum payment of their choosing.

> *"So they weighed out for my wages thirty pieces of silver."* (Zechariah 11:12)

The pay-off that Israel came up with was not some off-hand, arbitrary amount, nor was it just the excess change lying around. The number was representative of something else, and the hierarchy of Israel would have been perfectly aware of its implication when they arrived at the sum.

> *"If the ox gores a male or female servant, he shall give to their master thirty shekels of silver, and the ox shall be stoned."* (Exodus 21:32)

By Jewish law, if a slave was killed by an animal, the owner of the animal had to pay the slave's master thirty pieces of silver, and stone the animal to death.

Now, look at what the owner of the ox had to pay in the event that his animal killed someone's son or daughter:

> *"If there is imposed on him a sum of money, then he shall pay to redeem his life, whatever is imposed on him. Whether it has gored a son or gored a daughter, according to this judgment it shall be done to him."* (Exodus 21:30, 31)

There was no set monetary penalty for the death of a son or daughter. The amount owed by the animal's owner was an unspecified amount that had to be paid, "whatever is imposed on him." In other words, whatever the price a father demanded for the death of his child, one must pay if he wanted "to redeem his life." To set the price at thirty pieces of silver was to openly regard God as unfamiliar and as unimportant as a slave.

This was a divorce from God in *relational* terms. They were declaring that they did not want to be considered family, but preferred to view their time together as one views a dead servant. The time together was nice, but all things come to an end: time to move on.

Applying the thought to our modern times, what price could we give to pay God back for all He has done? No amount of money or devotion could ever be enough. Fortunately, we are not required to pay God back for any of His grace. The staff "Beauty" was broken as a symbol of the broken grace of His covenant with them. The moment they paid Him off with the thirty pieces of silver, the grace of a provisional covenant was gone.

When Israel Bought Their Way Out of Covenant

As we have established throughout this chapter, God can and did break covenant with Israel, based upon the prophecy of Zechariah 11. He is not in the habit of breaking covenant, as some covenants are specifically designated by the adjective "everlasting." This was a special moment, which our study revealed was fulfilled within the lifetime of Christ. The additional information about the thirty pieces of silver gives us a specific moment when the covenant relationship ended between God and Israel.

"Then one of the twelve, called Judas Iscariot, went to the chief priests and said, 'What are you willing to give me if I deliver Him to you?' And they counted out to him thirty pieces of silver. So from that time he sought opportunity to betray Him." (Matthew 26:14-16)

Just as thirty pieces of silver stood for a dead slave to a Hebrew, that same number represents the betrayal of the Lord Jesus to Christians. These two representations are not independent, but are connected forever. The prophecy existed when the chief priests set the price on Jesus' head and they were perfectly aware of what they were doing, even if Judas was not.

I personally believe that Judas was convinced Jesus was merely misunderstood, and needed an audience with the authorities in order to properly convey His case. I base this upon the fact that when he saw that Jesus was condemned, he turned remorseful and brought back the thirty pieces of silver to the chief priests and the elders (Matthew 27:3). Judas hanged himself in guilt, forever becoming the symbol of those who hang themselves with condemnation, oblivious that Jesus' hanging was done in their place.

The leaders of Israel that had worked so hard to put Jesus on a cross were not oblivious to the spiritual implications of their actions. They refused to take back the blood money that Judas had returned, instead purchasing the local potter's field in which to bury strangers (Matthew 27:7). The potter's field was the final resting place of the broken vessels which the potter had tossed out. How fitting, that the money used to betray our Lord was used to purchase a resting place for the broken and hurting. Even in His death, Jesus couldn't help but offer life!

This purchase of the potter's field was an intentional act of prophetic fulfillment as well. No other act, not even the thirty pieces of silver, proves more convincingly that the leaders of Christ's crucifixion wanted a complete severing of their relationship with God. Look at what Zechariah says should be done with the thirty pieces of silver:

"And the LORD said to me, 'Throw it to the potter' – that princely price they set on me. So I took the thirty pieces of silver and threw them into the house of the LORD for the potter." (Zechariah 11:13)

It Truly is Finished!

With the Old Covenant having its demands fulfilled by the life of Christ, categorized by His declaration of having finished the Father's work (John 17:4), it is now obliterated by another "It is finished." When Jesus finished the work at Calvary, His second finish was to break the covenant between the Father and Israel. The price of buying God off, prophesied as thirty pieces of silver, was paid in full. Jesus had done the work, and a new day was dawning.

When Christ resurrected, His new life was made possible by the Father's seal of approval on His Finished Work. The Old Covenant had no binding, and the Jewish economy was on its last leg. Within one generation, just as prophesied by Jesus, the temple would fall, the genealogical records would be burned, and the priesthood would be destroyed. The old rites and passages of a works-based religion were merely shells, combated by the many letters of the Apostle Paul and completely upended by the radical teachings of the Book of Hebrews. Christ appeared at the end of an age and put away sin by the sacrifice of Himself (Hebrews 9:26). With one covenant down, a new one could come on the scene.

We opened this chapter with an observation: so many Christians are confused in their walk with God because they are guilty of mixing the covenants. Having shown the lengths to which God went in order to sever His Old Covenant, why would we ever prop it up as a standard for righteousness? Why would we judge people based upon their performance rather than honor the age of a better covenant, where people are judged through the Finished Work?

Now we move forward into the glories of the New Covenant by looking back to that which it was modeled upon. Onward we go into a brave world of hope, with Jesus as our focal point and centerpiece. Prepare your hearts, for Jesus being in the center is nothing new. He has been there from the beginning, and the beauty of the covenant has always demanded it.

Chapter 8

Abraham and His Seed

In a previous chapter, we looked closely at Paul's insight into Calvary as brought to us through Galatians 3:13, "Christ has redeemed us from the curse of the law, having become a curse for us (for it is written, 'Cursed is everyone who hangs on a tree')." We shed light on both the power and the importance of this event, which gives us freedom from the past and the future.

Let's now dive in and take a look at where that particular verse leads us. The purpose for Christ being made a curse has been uncovered, but the widespread scope of such an event can be missed if we do not read on.

We have dealt extensively with Israel and her place in covenantal prophecy over the last several chapters. One might take our writings about Israel being forsaken, the Jewish leaders conspiring to crucify Jesus and God's breaking of covenant, as anti-Israel musings. However, nothing could be further from the truth. I am in no way against Israel, nor do I disrespect her position in the world. But I will not put Israel on a higher level than any other nation, nor do I believe God blesses her by any different ways or means than any other nation.

My reasoning for this is based, for the most part, on the next verse in sequence. Paul has told us about Christ being made a curse, and then he tells us why that is important:

"That the blessing of Abraham might come upon the Gentiles in Christ Jesus, that we might receive the promise of the Spirit through faith." (Galatians 3:14)

God's purpose for Calvary was to bring the blessings given to Abraham through the Abrahamic covenant to Gentile people. The Gentiles had no rights or privileges of covenant since they were not of the family of Abraham. The "family" was of supreme importance to the Jews (notice the Pharisees' pride in calling themselves, "children of Abraham"). Verse 14 tells us that the new requirement for Abraham's blessings was not to be a part of Abraham's lineage (seed), but to have faith in Jesus Christ.

This was a game-changer! God now had a means by which to pour out favor on the entire human family, not just one race or religion. Christ's death was certainly redemptive in terms of a Jew being freed from the law, but it was demonstrative in terms of the world actually knowing how much God loved them. The whole of humanity could have been restored to God with a single word, or with the wave of His hand, but only through the sacrificial death of His only begotten Son on the cross would mankind know and see what their Heavenly Father really felt towards them.

Actually, "game-changer" may not be the exact phrase that we need, for in reality God had always determined to bring about justification by faith. Paul brought out that Abraham had believed God and that his faith was counted to him for righteousness. "Therefore know that only those who are of faith are sons of Abraham. And the Scripture, foreseeing that God would justify the Gentiles by faith, preached the gospel to Abraham beforehand, saying, 'In you all the nations shall be blessed.' So then those who are of faith are blessed with believing Abraham" (Galatians 3:7-9). Notice that God's foresight was that He would justify the Gentiles "by faith." He wasn't necessarily changing the entire system at Calvary, He was just fulfilling what He had always wanted to do!

Equally incredible, is how world-changing Galatians 3:14 is in terms of man's equality to his fellow man. We have all heard the statement, "the ground is level at the foot of the cross," and this is even more remarkable when one considers how uneven that ground had been up until that point.

One Man from Two

Before Christ opened the way to the Father through faith in His finished work, the only people on earth with any legal claim to God were the Israelites, who had the commandments of the law and the provisions of the Mosaic Covenant to live by. They had a priesthood which represented them before God, and a sacrificial system by which they could approach Him for redemption. Everyone else was considered an outsider, a stranger, and a barbarian.

> "Therefore remember that you, once Gentiles in the flesh — who are called Uncircumcision by what is called the Circumcision made in the flesh by hands — that at that time you were without Christ, being aliens from the commonwealth of Israel and strangers from the covenants of promise, having no hope and without God in the world. But now in Christ Jesus you who once were far off have been brought near by the blood of Christ." (Ephesians 2:11-13)

Paul states the case: the first part is known by all Jews, that Gentiles are uncircumcised and therefore, without a covenant. Because they are without a covenant, they have no reason to hope, for they do not know God. The second part was revolutionary, for it declared that those same strangers and aliens are now just as near to God as any Jew always claimed to be, and all because of "the blood of Christ."

> "For He Himself is our peace, who has made both one, and has broken down the middle wall of separation." (Ephesians 2:14)

Good news from abroad is not our peace. Having more money than we have debt is not our peace. Being healthy while others are sick is not our peace. Christ Himself is our peace! His peace has made two separate peoples into one. The Jew and the Gentile no longer have a wall of division between them. In God's eyes, the wall is gone.

> "Having abolished in His flesh the enmity, that is, the law of commandments contained in ordinances, so as to create in Himself one new man from the two, thus making peace, and that He might

reconcile them both to God in one body through the cross, thereby putting to death the enmity." (Ephesians 2:15, 16)

Once Christ abolished the enemy, which was the law, He was able to create one new man (church) out of two (Jews and Gentiles). This reconciled the entire world to God through Christ's death on the cross, finishing off the power of the law.

The Changeless Promise

"Brethren, I speak in the manner of men: Though it is only a man's covenant, yet if it is confirmed, no one annuls or adds to it." (Galatians 3:15)

Using an example from the natural realm, Paul is preparing us for a spiritual revelation. If two men enter into a covenant, and they confirm that covenant with the requisite sacrifice of blood, then no one can add or take away from the terms and conditions of that covenant. In other words, once a covenant was cut, there was no outside influence that could change it in any way.

"Now to Abraham and his Seed were the promises made. He does not say, 'And to seeds,' as of many, but as of one, 'And to your Seed,' who is Christ." (Galatians 3:16)

Notice the capitalization used in this particular translation of the word "Seed," making it a proper noun. This is confirmed in the second half of the verse by a comparison of what the Lord *did not* say versus what He *did* say. He does not give promises to Abraham's natural children, but to one specific heir, whom Paul recognizes as Christ.

This sheds a different light on the famous promise of blessings and curses that God gave to Abraham when He called him out of Ur to make of him "a great nation":

"I will bless those who bless you, and I will curse him who curses you; and in you all the families of the earth shall be blessed." (Genesis 12:3)

Part of the promise appears to be corporate; "...bless those," while part seems individual; "...curse him." Without reading too much into the pronoun usage, one can make a case that even here there is a reference to a "him" being made the curse, which could point to Christ, and Him being made a curse on the cross.

Either way, Galatians 3:16 sets the stage for all of the Abrahamic promises to be realized through Christ rather than through someone's family heritage or bloodline.

No Interference by the Law

> *"And this I say, that the law, which was four hundred and thirty years later, cannot annul the covenant that was confirmed before by God in Christ, that it should make the promise of no effect."* (Galatians 3:17)

The law referred to in Verse 17, the Law of Moses, was given at Sinai to the children of Israel, approximately 50 days after they left the land of Egypt. This first Pentecost marked the beginning of the age of the Mosaic Economy, which would last until the fall of the final Jewish temple in Jerusalem in AD 70. The law arrived 430 years after God made the initial promise to Abraham and his "Seed," and could not take away from the promises of that initial covenant.

This verse states that God's covenant with Abraham could not be overruled by His covenant with Israel. The result of the covenant with Abraham was a promise that God would bless His Seed and that through Him, "all the families of the earth" would be blessed. This covenant is often referred to as "The Covenant of Promise." The Mosaic Law could not take away the power of that promise, meaning that God was going to keep that promise, regardless of how Israel responded under the law.

> *"For if the inheritance is of the law, it is no longer of promise; but God gave it to Abraham by promise."* (Galatians 3:18)

It is important for us to at least attempt to get inside the mindset of those Jews to whom the Mosaic Law had been given. Having had over four centuries of familiarity with the covenant that God made with Abraham, they are confronted at Sinai by an entirely new concept, in which they are blessed or cursed based upon their obedience. They believed that the Mosaic Law now took precedence over the Abrahamic covenant – in their mind, why else would God have added it in? Paul's argument in Galatians 3 is an attempt to flip that concept around. It is actually the covenant that takes priority over the law, which was added later, and was *only temporary*.

Please take a closer look at that last sentence. If the concept was hard for the Jew to understand, it may be even harder for the modern Christian. We have built most of the forms of our Christianity around a code of conduct and a fearful expectation of swift retribution if we either break the rules or if we even *want* to break the rules. In fact, most Christians live out a lifestyle that is actually worse than the Jews had it under the law. At least under Mosaic Law man could *feel* differently than he was performing and he thought he was fine since he hadn't actually *done* something wrong. Under "grace" and "New Covenant," most Christians carry guilt and condemnation over the fact that they *feel* or *think* sinfully. My point is that most believers are so Mosaic Law-minded, rather than Abrahamic Covenant-minded, that they struggle with the concept of that law being temporary and they keep themselves in a performance-based religion rather than an inheritance-based relationship.

A Promised Inheritance

Verse 18 identifies what the Covenant of Promise was actually promising: an inheritance. That inheritance didn't come by the keeping of the law, but by a decree of heaven. Abraham was a recipient of the inheritance simply because he believed he was promised an inheritance. He found this out in the natural realm by taking inventory of his life and accounting the source of his blessings. Paul said it this way:

> "What then shall we say that Abraham our father has found according to the flesh? For if Abraham was justified by works, he has something to boast about, but not before God. For what does the Scripture say? 'Abraham believed God, and it was accounted to him

*for righteousness.' Now to him who works, the wages are not counted
as grace but as debt."* (Romans 4:1-4)

Abrahams' justification, or right-standing before God, had nothing to do
with whether or not he lived perfectly; he believed God when God made him
a promise. He knew that his inheritance was a *grace* inheritance and not one of
debt. In fact, the book of Genesis records Abraham as being less than perfect and
still receiving the fullness of God's blessings (see Genesis 12:10-20 and Genesis
20:1-18 in which Abraham makes the same mistake *twice* and does not receive
a reprimand, instead he receives a blessing!)

An inheritance cannot, by definition, be enhanced or diminished by works. It
is due to the recipient on the grounds that he is the legal family heir. To try and
receive an inheritance by works or by earning it is to deny one's place as a family
member and to instead prefer to receive it based upon performance. This is paramount to a son surrendering his right to the family fortune so that he can earn
that same fortune through his performance. We Americans tend to applaud such
efforts because we have a Hollywood mentality. In our "two-hour movie" minds,
it makes for great drama to imagine a young man refusing to inherit the com-
pany that his father has built for him, opting rather to work his way up from the
bottom so he can earn it. This fundamental misunderstanding of the beauty of
inheritance is nothing new. Jesus encountered the fallacy in His ministry as well.

*"Now a certain ruler asked him, saying, "Good Teacher, what shall I
do to inherit eternal life?"* (John 18:18)

The story of the Rich Young Ruler rotates around a bizarre question: What
must I *do* to *inherit* eternal life? I emphasize the two words that do not go
together. One cannot "do" anything to merit what is his by inheritance. This
confusion causes the young man to seek a salvation by works, and to leave Jesus
empty-handed. His lack of salvation cannot be blamed on the Master, for there
is NO salvation to be found for any of us by our works or our merit.

Purpose of the Law

"What purpose then does the law serve? It was added because of transgressions, till the Seed should come to whom the promise was made; and it was appointed through angels by the hand of a mediator." (Galatians 3:19)

Straightforward and simple, Paul asks, and then answers, the question that so many have debated for centuries: "What purpose does the law serve?" The reason for the debate may have to do with how little he gives in response to such a loaded question. We should also point to an apparent contradiction in another Pauline epistle that forces us to deal with this in more depth. Remembering that Galatians states that the law was added "because of transgressions," we look at another statement regarding the law in Paul's letter to the Romans.

"For if those who are of the law are heirs, faith is made void and the promise made of no effect, because the law brings about wrath; for <u>where there is no law there is no transgression</u>." (Romans 4:14, 15)

The first half of the verse parallels what we have seen revealed in the Book of Galatians regarding faith and the promise. The portion of scripture that I underlined shows us a contrast to Paul's Galatians statement that the law was added because of transgressions. Here, in Romans, Paul says that where the law doesn't exist, there is no transgression. Which one is correct? Is the law to show the transgression or is the transgression non-existent without the law? The answer is in the context, and in reality, the answer is "Both are correct!"

Let's deal with the Romans scripture first, and within the context of the writing. Paul states that the promise that Abraham would be the heir of the world was not to him or his seed through the law, but through the righteousness of faith (Romans 4:13). Abraham's promise of inheritance belonged to him because he believed it, not because he obeyed the law. Paul then argues that if a man receives the inheritance because he keeps the law, then there is no need for faith and an inheritance by promise is null and void. It is interesting to note that faith is not necessary for the keeping of the law. Then again, why would it be? Just obey and receive. You need not believe or trust, only DO or DON'T DO whatever the list of commands requires. Truthfully, the more you live by the law, the less you operate in faith, and the more you function by sight.

The proper interpretation of "where there is no law there is no transgression" can be found in understanding the first half of the verse in which "the law brings about wrath." God's wrath against sin was brought about because the law was being broken. If those who are of the law are heirs, then God doesn't look for your faith (because your faith is worthless) and there is no need to make you any promises (because your lack of keeping the law will render any promise useless anyhow). This brings about the wrath of God on Israel, since they were no longer looking to be dealt with by promise but by obedience. That concludes with the statement, "where there is no law there is no transgression," meaning that if they were not under the Mosaic Law, there would be no need for God to display wrath and they could still receive the promise by faith. In other words, the law was an interruption.

Paul completes the thought in the next chapter when trying to explain how sin entered the world and death piggy-backed in on it.

> *"For until the law sin was in the world, but sin is not imputed when there is no law."* (Romans 5:13)

Imputation, or accounting, of sin comes about because the one who is sinning is under a law that forbids it. If there were no law forbidding it, there would be no sin to charge to the person. That puts a fine point on Paul's phrase "where there is no law there is no transgression."

Now we come to our text in Galatians, in which it appears that God WAS counting Israel's sins under the Abrahamic covenant and because they piled up, He brought the law to Moses to show Israel how bad she was. However, this can't be possible in light of Romans 4:15: thus the "transgressions" that Israel is guilty of, that prompts the arrival of the law, must be something aside from these things we call "sin," under the law.

Don't forget the one act that Israel was required to do under the Abrahamic covenant: only believe. If they could just believe, God would do the rest. This is why Paul spends the first few verses of Romans 4 explaining how Abraham was made righteous simply by his faith.

The great "Hall of Faith," recorded in Hebrews 11, gives at least 17 instances of Old Testament characters doing things "by faith." Take a look at that chapter on your own, concentrating on Verses 4 through the end of the chapter. You will see faith in action, as the old saints believed God for great things. From Abel to Moses, the list contains some of the mighty acts of faith by some of history's greatest characters.

Of the 17 instances recorded in that brief span of history in Hebrews 11, a startling 15 of them come before the giving of the law on Mt. Sinai. There is not one story recorded regarding a mighty act of faith between the crossing of the Red Sea into the wilderness and the final crossing of the Jordan into the land of promise. That is a silent span of nearly 40 years, which the author of Hebrews skips, opting to take the reader to the walls of Jericho, and to a harlot named Rahab. That same period of time takes up an enormous chunk of our Pentateuch (first 5 books of the Bible), namely from Exodus 15 through Joshua 5. What Hebrews is teaching us is that faith was in operation from the beginning of the biblical story up until the giving of the law on Sinai. Then, faith comes back on the scene in the Promised Land.

The Promised Land was what Israel had been waiting on forever! This was the guarantee that God had given to their father, Abraham, that they would possess "all the land of Canaan" (Genesis 17:8). Why is it that there is mighty faith recorded around every turn from Abel to the Red Sea, and then silence until Israel arrives in that Promised Land? The answer is the key to Galatians 3:19.

In the immediate aftermath of the great Red Sea miracle, Moses and Israel sing a song of rejoicing and celebration (Exodus 15). Take a moment and review that song; it drips with faith and power! Three days later, Israel arrives in the Wilderness of Shur (Shur is the Hebrew word for "wall;" note how differently they handle this first "wall" compared to the walls of Jericho in the Promised Land). They encounter the bitter waters of a place called Marah, and they begin to complain (Exodus 15:24). So begins a trend in which a people once so full of faith and confidence now trade that faith for fear and unbelief.

After Marah, Israel complains because they are hungry, and then at Rephidim they fear they will die of thirst. Their attitude of rest and faith all but gone, they finally tempt the Lord by saying, "Is the LORD among us or not?" (Exodus 17:7).

God had called Israel out; first from the world at large, and then from the land of Egypt, so that He could have for Himself a "kingdom of priests and a holy nation" (Exodus 19:6). By definition, a priest is a representative of man to God. By declaring His intention to make all of Israel a kingdom of priests, God is displaying His plan for the ages; that Israel would represent planet earth and its inhabitants before Heaven. Through her, God would bless all the nations of the earth. There would be no need for individual priests within Israel, for there would be no Israelite that felt any distance or separation from God. This was Heaven's stroke of equality and salvation.

As great as God's plan for mankind was, Israel continued her gradual sliding into a works-based mentality rather than a faith-based one. Eventually they gave up on the original promise of inheritance and challenged God that they could do whatever He demanded of them (this is the Hebrew rendering of Israel's approval of the law in Exodus 19:8). Their first encounter with God at Sinai completes their forfeit of the promise as they beg Moses to speak on their behalf (Exodus 20:19; Hebrews 12:19).

Destined to be a kingdom of priests, Israel surrenders her intimacy with God, and rejects His affections. This rejection is the transgression that Paul is speaking of in Galatians 3:19. Because Israel had moved their faith away from the promise made to Abraham and onto their own ability, God gave them the law so they could try and please Him through their works. Many modern answers to "What is the purpose of the law?" include statements about God needing to show man how to live, or to establish a higher moral code. These answers simply ignore the fact that God had dealt with mankind without that law for centuries, and He seemed to have no problem blessing them.

Israel exchanged a relationship for a religion, and the cold, harsh distance that they place between them and their God of deliverance culminates in them believing that God hates them (Deuteronomy 1:27). No nation could fall so far as the one who creates a distance between herself and her Creator, and then believes that distance to be evidence of God's disdain.

Till the Seed Should Come

"What purpose then does the law serve? It was added because of transgressions, till the Seed should come to whom the promise was made; and it was appointed through angels by the hand of a mediator." (Galatians 3:19)

The second part of Paul's answer to the question of what purpose the law serves is, "till the Seed should come to whom the promise was made." Verse 16 identified that "Seed" as Christ, which means that the law served its purpose until Jesus. This coincides perfectly with Christ's statement that He did not come to destroy the law but to fulfill (Matthew 5:17). It did not need to be destroyed; it needed to be fulfilled, much like the note on your house doesn't need to be destroyed (that wouldn't do any good!), it just needs to be paid off.

Again, though risking redundancy, what purpose can the law serve for a believer under the New Covenant, now that the Seed has come? Christ was the one to whom the promises of the Abrahamic Covenant were made. It is all fulfilled in Him, placing Him at the center of it all.

As we stated a few paragraphs ago, God called Israel out of the world to be a kingdom of priests. However, we know they failed to fulfill that destiny because they did not believe. In fact, the gospel (good news) that had been preached to them, which stated that they would inherit a Promised Land, did not profit them, "not being mixed with faith in those who heard it" (Hebrews 4:2). In order for the promise of an inheritance to do Israel any good, they had to mix faith with what they were hearing.

Christ's death at Calvary was a pre-ordained event, determined by God to occur (Revelation 13:8). He was "foreordained before the foundation of the world, but was manifest in these last times for you" (1 Peter 1:20). It is important to see this, as it shows us that Calvary was NOT God's response to the problems of mankind. He KNEW that His first Adam would fail. He KNEW that His chosen people Israel would fail and He KNEW that if He were to move into the human timeline in the form of a man, literally make the Word become flesh, then He would be able to fulfill things and inherit the fullness. He may have lost His nation of priests when Israel rejected Him, but He gained a Great High

Priest through Jesus. Furthermore, though Christ, God has made His church into a kingdom of priests (Revelation 1:6), finally achieving in us, what He never achieved in Israel. Believe me, it isn't our doing. The Finished Work of our Savior is simply that good!

In short, Calvary was not a reaction. Calvary was THE action!

By the Hand of a Mediator

"…and it was appointed through angels by the hand of a mediator."
(Galatians 3:19)

When Israel surrendered their position as a kingdom of priests, they chose Moses to represent them to God. The key text that is used to support this idea seems to indicate that Israel was choosing Moses to represent God to the people rather than the other way around. Notice the wording:

"Then they said to Moses, 'You speak with us, and we will hear; but let not God speak with us, lest we die." (Exodus 20:19)

Paul states that the law was added to Israel "by the hand of a mediator," and we know that mediator was Moses, as John said, "The law was given by Moses" (John 1:17). Next, Paul pins down who the mediator was actually representing, in spite of how the wording appears in Exodus 20:19.

"Now a mediator does not mediate for one only, but God is one."
(Galatians 3:20)

A mediator is not necessary if there is only one person to represent, since that person could simply speak on his own behalf. When large numbers of people are involved, one mediator or representative has to speak for the entire group. When Paul emphasizes that there is no mediator for "one only," he follows it up with "but God is one." His point is that the mediator is representing the people to God, not the other way around.

This means that Israel really was asking Moses to be their representative in front of God. They were surrendering their priestly status in order to allow Moses the glory of standing in the presence of heaven.

Jesus has become our mediator, representing the whole of humanity to the one Father. The author of Hebrews, after establishing that the blood of bulls and goats and the ashes of a heifer could only purify the outside, states that the blood of Jesus could "cleanse your conscience from dead works to serve the living God" (Hebrews 9:14).

> "And for this reason He is the Mediator of the new covenant by means of death, for the redemption of the transgressions under the first covenant, that those who are called may receive the promise of the eternal inheritance." (Hebrews 9:15)

Jesus mediates the new covenant "by means of death," placing Calvary at the center of everything related to redemption. His death was for the sins committed under the first covenant, meaning those committed under the law. Those are the sins that required redemption of blood, for they were the cause of man's evil conscience.

Consequently, mankind STILL carries an evil conscience over his failures under the law. If we could bring people to a revelation that they are not under the law and that anything committed against that law has been paid for, they would begin to live the life of happy abundance and rest in the Finished Work.

The Law vs. The Promise?

> "Is the law then against the promises of God? Certainly not! For if there had been a law given which could have given life, truly righteousness would have been by the law." (Galatians 3:21)

Is there a battle between the promise and the law? Or, worded a bit closer to our modern way of speaking, as The Message tends to do: "If such is the case, is the law, then, an anti-promise, a negation of God's will for us?" Paul answers emphatically, "Certainly not!" The law could not give life to those who kept it, for if it were even possible for it to do so then righteousness would have come through keeping the law. Remember, Jesus was not righteous because He kept the law to perfection. Jesus was righteous because He was declared to be so by the Father. His baptism in the Jordan was to "fulfill all righteousness," and it prompted the Father to say, "I am well pleased" (Matthew 3:15, 17).

If God's plan for mankind was to move into Him and develop relationship, then a promised land was not even enough. He did not want mankind to simply dwell on a piece of real estate. He wanted heaven's real estate to dwell in man! The law simply declared the world guilty and shut man's mouth of self-righteousness (Romans 3:19). They could have had all that God wanted for them by only believing Him for it and trusting Him implicitly. However, they failed in that and went under the yoke of bondage that is the law (Galatians 5:1). Therefore, I hope you can see that the law was NEVER meant to make a man righteous, nor was it to replace the promise of inheritance to the "Seed." It's end result is displayed in Paul's next verse:

> "But the Scripture has confined all under sin, that the promise of faith in Jesus Christ might be given to those who believe." (Galatians 3:22)

The law did its job in that it confined the whole of humanity beneath the burden of sin, so that the promise of salvation though Jesus Christ by simple faith, could be given to all believers. Where man rejected a relationship of promise through Abraham's covenant and exchanged it for a religion of works under Mosaic Law, Jesus Christ brings the world back into relationship through faith in His Finished Work.

Kept Under Guard

Like a prisoner who has a guard assigned to him day and night, Israel had the guardian of the Mosaic Law. It was to last until the arrival of faith.

> "But before faith came, we were kept under guard by the law, kept for the faith which would afterward be revealed. Therefore the law was

our tutor to bring us to Christ, that we might be justified by faith."
(Galatians 3:23, 24)

The words "to bring us" are italicized in the Authorized Version of the Bible and are not found in the original Greek manuscript. They are added words, placed there by translators to help further the thought and fill in the gaps. In this particular case, I think they actually *detract* from the thought, aiming us in the wrong direction. The law was not given "to bring us" to Christ, but rather, "the law was our tutor to Christ." It was all that we had until Christ came. The intent of Paul's statement is not to insinuate that the law is what people need until they get to Christ (they are actually under some sort of *performance-based* system before they come to Christ anyway). He is saying that the law was to tutor Israel until Christ came to be their teacher.

> *"But after faith has come, we are no longer under a tutor."* (Galatians 3:25)

Joint Heirs

> *"For you are all sons of God through faith in Christ Jesus...And if you are Christ's, then you are Abraham's seed, and heir according to the promise."* (Galatians 3:26, 29)

Nothing could be more jarring to a Jew than Paul's closing argument of Galatians 3. He has declared sonship on all who profess faith in Christ Jesus, going so far as to shatter the distinction between Jew and Greek, slave and free, and male and female in Verse 28. The icing on the cake is the final verse, in which Paul unequivocally pronounces that if man has placed faith in Christ, then he is the seed of Abraham. Remember a bit earlier in the chapter when Paul said that the "seed" to whom the Abrahamic promises were made was Christ? He now states that if man is in Christ then he is also that seed.

If Christ is the Seed and you are the seed, then you are an heir of the promise. In Romans 8:17, Paul says that if we are the children of God then we are heirs of whatever He has and indeed are joint-heirs with Christ. Whatever you identify as belonging to Christ, now also belongs to you!

God Saw You at Calvary

I remember a song from my youth that would often be performed in church as a special solo. It spoke of the moment when Jesus was on the cross and how there was a look of love on His face. The chorus stated that when He was on the cross, we were on His mind. I know the imagery of that is powerful, but it may become even more so when we realize that we were not only on His mind, but we were in His eyes.

> *"Yet it pleased the LORD to bruise Him; He has put Him to grief. When You make His soul an offering for sin, He shall see His seed, He shall prolong His days, and the pleasure of the LORD shall prosper in His hand."* (Isaiah 53:10)

When Jesus was being offered up for the sin of the world, the Father saw His seed. Since Jesus had no natural children (Verse 8 of that chapter attests to that), the seed that the Father saw at Calvary must be all of those who would place faith in that Finished Work. We were in the eyes of the Father as He looked down upon His Son.

One more interesting fact about Isaiah 53:10 that makes for a wonderful conclusion to this chapter is found in another italicized word. "He shall prolong His days," reads differently in Hebrew, for there is a word that was not originally there. It should say, "He shall prolong days." While this may seem insignificant, it only makes sense that the word really does not belong, seeing as Jesus' days were not prolonged at Calvary.

The "seed" that God saw was you and me, thus the days that He is prolonging are our days. We can begin to tap into yet another promise of sonship; that Christ's death has paid for our life. Remember, the only one that gains in death is the one who dies, but for us to live is to show forth our Redeemer every moment.

> *"For to me, to <u>live</u> is Christ, and to die is gain."* (Philippians 1:21)

Chapter 9

Two Immutable Things

We have gathered several thoughts from the book of Hebrews many times over the course of the last few chapters. This book's message of Christ as superior to all others was aimed primarily at Jews who had come to the saving knowledge of Jesus and who were tempted to go back to the outward forms of temple worship. The author's arguments are rich and full of details that are difficult to sum up in even the most complex writings. He attempted to sum it up in the first verses of Chapter 8:

> *"Now this is the main point of the things we are saying: We have such a High Priest, who is seated at the right hand of the throne of the Majesty in the heavens, a Minister of the sanctuary and of the true tabernacle which the Lord erected, and not man."* (Hebrews 8:1, 2)

It is not that we *had* a high priest, but rather, we *have* a High Priest (note the capitalization, which indicates more than a title). He is currently seated at the right hand of God in the realm of the heavenly dimension.

> *"But now He has obtained a more excellent ministry, inasmuch as He is also Mediator of a better covenant, which was established on better promises."* (Hebrews 8:6)

Christ is no longer operating in the system of "gifts and sacrifices" (Hebrews 8:3), but has now obtained a more excellent ministry. He is the Mediator of a better covenant, but better than what covenant? The writer is obviously referring to the covenant in which earthly priests were necessary, which excludes the one with Abraham, and perfectly defines the Old Covenant given at Sinai. This "better covenant" was established on a better set of promises than those of the Mosaic Law. The Old Covenant promised that if you did well, God would bless you, but if you did poorly, God would curse you. Jesus is the Mediator of the New Covenant, which promises that all things are yours "for Christ's sake."

> "For there is one God and one Mediator between God and men, the Man Christ Jesus." (1 Timothy 2:5)

Remember that God is one (Galatians 3:20), Jesus is the Mediator, and we are many, thus the use of the plural form "men." Jesus' role as Mediator is founded in His Finished Work which He accomplished as a man. By dying as a man, He could taste death for us, and ratify the covenant before the Father.

> "I desire therefore that the men pray everywhere, lifting up holy hands, without wrath and doubting." (1 Timothy 2:8)

The word "therefore" appears because of Verse 5. Since there is one God and one Mediator between God and men, all men should pray. Their hands are holy, and they can lift them without fear of God's wrath and without doubting His love. This confidence is only possible when we see Jesus as our Mediator, and we believe that God is viewing Him instead of us.

Faith Without Works

As we stated earlier, *Hebrews* was written to Jews who were followers of Christ but who were leaning towards a return to the law and the practices of Judaism. It seems so obvious to us, 2000 years beyond the cross, that Jesus is the only way to the Father, and we find it difficult to fathom how anyone could go back to temple worship, offering of sacrifices, observing certain holy days, etc. However, to the Jews of that day, the Mosaic Law was so engrained in them as being a means of righteousness, that to abandon it felt like an abandonment of Moses himself. This was treasonous, and only those sold out to the cause of Christ could bring themselves to such a state.

This is the reason that James wrote his controversial little letter "to the twelve tribes scattered abroad" (James 1:1), and it might also be the reason why it was placed just after Hebrews in the ordering of the New Testament. The Jewish people living in the Roman Empire had a national exemption from the Roman law which commanded that all of its citizens had to call Caesar "god." Rome allowed Jews to call Yahweh, "God," and not be punished by Rome for treason. When Christianity began to take hold in the Roman Empire, followers of Christ refused to surrender their belief that Jesus, not Caesar, was God. No such exemption existed for Christians, thus they were under penalty of imprisonment or perhaps death if they refused to call Caesar "god."

Some Jewish Christians were claiming Christ right until the point of the sword, when they would deny both Christ and Caesar in claiming only Yahweh as their God. This kept them safe from Roman retribution, but not from the wrathful pen of the Apostle James. His question, "What does it profit if someone says he has faith but does not have works?" (James 2:14) is not a call for a works-based salvation, but rather a call for Jewish Christians to show their faith on a day-to-day basis. They could believe there was but "one God," and be no better off than demons (James 2:19), for their silence about Jesus being that one God prompted him to write that their faith was dead (James 2:25).

Through the depth of the book of Hebrews, and the arguments of the Apostle James, I hope you can see that a works-based salvation is no better than an Old Covenant. Conversely, a salvation based only upon words, with no deeds to confirm them, was the same old death in new packaging.

Confirmed By God, in Christ

Having already established that the law, which came 430 years after the promise to Abraham, could not annul that promise, Paul stated that the Abrahamic covenant was confirmed before God, "in Christ" (Galatians 3:17). This is an interesting statement, since Jesus came centuries after the Abrahamic Covenant.

We could take the phrase "in Christ" to mean that God was putting His seal of approval on the Abrahamic Covenant through the sacrificial death of His Son. However, that would have God waiting until the end of the Mosaic Law to confirm the covenant that came *before* the law. This is a possibility, but it seems secondary at best.

Primarily, we must assume according to Galatians 3:17, that Christ was actually present at the cutting of the Abrahamic Covenant. While most believers would readily admit that wherever God was active in the Old Testament, Jesus was certainly there, it is slightly more difficult to wrap our minds around the fact that He was there in more than spirit. In other words, Christ was actually there.

Think of it in terms of Christ being eternal, having neither a start nor a finish. The author of Hebrews compares the priesthood of Christ on par with Melchizedek of Genesis, in that neither had "beginning of days nor end of life" (Hebrews 7:3). We know that Jesus had a beginning of days on earth, as the Christmas story confirms, and we are also sure of the end of His life, as the story of Calvary bears out. In that last sentence lies the essence of the argument. Christ is eternal, but Jesus had a beginning and an end *on earth*.

> *"In the beginning was the Word, and the Word was with God, and the Word was God. He was in the beginning with God. All things were made through Him, and without Him nothing was made that was made."* (John 1:1-3)

John opens his gospel in the same way the Torah begins, with "In the beginning." John is introducing the reader to a new beginning, where Adam is now victorious instead of a failure. He calls Him, "the Word," stating that He was with God and was, in fact, God Himself. As the chapter unfolds, John puts flesh onto that Word:

> *"And the Word became flesh and dwelt among us, and we beheld His glory, the glory as of the only begotten of the Father, full of grace and truth."* (John 1:14)

The same Word from verse 1, which was always in existence, put on human flesh "and dwelt among us." He was the "only begotten of the Father," meaning that the Word had always been alive in the realm of the spirit, but was now alive in the realm of the natural. The Christ had become "Jesus," voluntarily placing Himself into the timeline of humanity so that He could sympathize with the plight of man, and personify the love of God.

This is another reason it is so important to take our image of God from what we see in Jesus. Jesus was the Christ, wrapped in a suit of flesh. When we begin to apply this idea to our Bible study, we have no problem seeing Christ around every turn in the Old Testament. We don't see the name 'Jesus', for He wouldn't be known by that name until Mary conceived of the Holy Spirit and bore Him at the Nativity. The Old Testament pictures are of Christ, and that contributes to our understanding of God's covenant.

We will look at the covenant cut with Abraham in more detail in the next chapter, and we will see exactly how Christ was involved. We will also find in what way the cross was a confirmation of that covenant. To get us there, we must look closely at one more vital passage from Hebrews which shows us God's infallible purpose in Christ.

God Swore By Himself

"For when God made a promise to Abraham, because He could swear by no one greater, He swore by Himself, saying, 'Surely blessing I will bless you, and multiplying I will multiply you.'" (Hebrews 6:13-14)

When someone wants to put an ironclad seal on a proclamation or a promise, they might say, "I swear on a stack of Bibles!" Meant as a reference to a courtroom witness swearing on the Bible to tell the truth, the "stack" apparently makes their oath all the more binding.

The "swear" is also done because what we are saying is unbelievable, and we need to lend some authenticity. Notice that those who are prone to being distrusted tend to swear they are telling the truth even more. Their reputation of tall tales precedes them, and they feel the need to swear to their honesty.

God does not have such a reputation. He IS truth, and His truth is not affected by our unbelief, is it?

"Certainly not! Indeed, let God be true but every man a liar." (Romans 3:4)

For God to swear cannot be because He has a reputation for dishonesty, but because the promise is so unbelievable. Thus, "Surely blessing I will bless you, and multiplying I will multiply you." Surely, or certainly, or "I swear," it will be done!

Patient Endurance

"And so, after he had patiently endured, he obtained the promise." (Hebrews 6:15)

Heaven does not run on Earth's time clock. Even as God was marking the days of creation before He created the sun, which marks time on earth, He was showing us that in the heavenly realm, His clock comes first. If a day is as a thousand years, and a thousand years is as a day, then one can be assured that in God, time is irrelevant.

Patient endurance on Abraham's part guaranteed he would obtain what was promised. Any doubt that it would be his would lead him to interject his own efforts in order to help the promise along. In fact, that's exactly what he did when he slept with the slave girl Hagar who bore him Ishmael. Ishmael was a product of the flesh, needing no supernatural help for conception. This interjection certainly slowed down the process of inheritance, but even that did not derail God's honesty in providing the promise.

Abraham first received the promise in Genesis 12, and Scripture reported him being 75 years old. Isaac, the son of promise (literally, the fulfillment), was born to him in Genesis 21, when Abraham was 100 years old. A gap of 25 years between the promise and its fulfillment, with unnecessary intervention in the meantime, shows us Abraham's "patient endurance." The author of Hebrews seems to ignore the Hagar/Ishmael incident, perhaps to teach us where God's focus was the entire time: on His promise, not on Abraham's actions.

"For men indeed swear by the greater, and an oath for confirmation is for them an end of all dispute." (Hebrews 6:16)

The end of dispute and discussion between two parties comes when each side has agreed on an oath. The confirmation for that oath was typically the cutting of covenant, which involved animal sacrifice, the giving of gifts and the sharing of a meal. While we sign contracts in modern times, the covenant of oath in ancient days would have been considered far more binding, since something lost its life in the transaction.

The Immutability of His Counsel

"Thus God, determining to show more abundantly to the heirs of promise the immutability of His counsel, confirmed it by an oath." (Hebrews 6:17)

God is truth, and has no need for a covenant in order to obligate Himself to keep His word. However, due to the fact that His covenant is with fallen, disloyal man, God ties Himself to His promise by cutting a covenant. This verse tells us that God was only doing this to "show more abundantly...the immutability of His counsel."

The word "immutability," and "immutable," found in Verse 18 are translated from the Greek word "ametathetos," which means, "Not transposed, not to be transferred, fixed, unalterable." It is the opposite of a word that appears in the next chapter in Hebrews, when the author states, "For the priesthood being changed, of necessity there is also a change of the law" (Hebrews 7:12). The word "changed," is the opposite of "immutability," meaning that the immutability of His counsel denotes an unchanging purpose.

Catch the importance of that statement: God was determined to show the heirs of His promise how unchangeable that promise was. Nothing could change God's mind about blessing His people on the basis of inheritance. Not even the advent of the law could change God's mind! This is further confirmation that the interruption by the Mosaic Law was always intended to be temporary.

Guaranteed By an Oath

The confirmation – guarantee – of God's purpose and promise was found in the oath He makes with Abraham. This oath is evident in the form of a covenant. Before we investigate that covenant fully, and see exactly how it came about, it is fitting to examine all that the oath of His promise represented.

When Zacharias circumcised his baby boy, John the Baptist, he was filled with the Holy Spirit and began to prophesy. He started by blessing the Lord and praising Him for visiting and redeeming Israel by giving them a "horn of salvation," from the "house of His servant David." Of course this prophecy was about Jesus, who was yet to be born.

He then confirmed that God had indeed spoken to His people for years through the mouths of the prophets and promised to save His people from the hands of their enemies. Then, he took his listeners back to a covenant.

> *"To perform the mercy promised to our fathers and to remember His*
> *holy covenant, the oath which He swore to our father Abraham".*
> (Luke 1:72, 73)

Most of us think the covenant that Jesus came to reinforce was the Mosaic Covenant, but Zacharias stated He came to perform the promise sworn to Abraham. This rewinds us beyond the giving of the law at Sinai and all the way to Genesis 12, where God swears to Abraham, which we just saw reiterated in Hebrews 6. Jesus' ministry was not to put man under the strain and demand of the law (man was *already* under that strain), but to take us back to a covenant of promise in which God blessed us by faith and not works.

Israel had functioned for so long within a works-based economy that a return to simple faith seemed not only treasonous, but also a bit lazy. The law had become their religion, and religion involves rules, regulations and formulas. Outward observance of standards replaced an inward change, and men became more impressed by clothing, scripture memorization and asceticism (strict self-denial as a form of spiritual discipline) than with a heart of faith. This is the primary cause for the Pharisee's vocal rejection of the miracles of Jesus. No matter how much "good" was coming out of His encounters with the blind, the lame, the leprous, the prostitutes and even the dead, He wasn't following the strict, outward code that defined their standards of purity and holiness.

Paul latched on to this concept with such clarity when addressing the issue of legalism to his church at Colosse:

> *"Therefore, if you died with Christ from the basic principles of the world, why, as though living in the world, do you subject yourselves to regulations – 'Do not touch, do not taste, do not handle,' which all concern things which perish with the using – according to the commandments and doctrines of men? These things indeed have an appearance of wisdom in self-imposed religion, false humility, and neglect of the body, but are of no value against the indulgence of the flesh."* (Colossians 2:20-23)

The "self-imposed religion" had replaced harmonious relationship. It produced a "false humility" through "neglect of the body," but it did nothing to change the person on the inside. Fear of rebellion and blatant sin kept the Pharisees from releasing the people into liberty, just as it keeps some church leaders from preaching and proclaiming liberty over the congregants through today. We fear the younger brother running off into a strange country to waste his inheritance on riotous living so much that we actually prefer the self-righteous, snobbish, judgmental, works-based attitude of the elder brother. Though we know it is not admirable to like him, many can't help but think that it's better to stay at home and work for daddy than to run off to the hog pen of the world. Truthfully, neither son understood the Father's love, nor did they have a revelation of sonship.

Walking according to the Spirit - impossible under the Old Covenant with its mandatory introspection - is the ultimate goal of the New Covenant experience. Serving as a temporary measure, the law implemented a life of rules and regulations in exchange for the beautiful relationship that Israel was so willing to surrender. With the Finished Work as our guide, we can now live according to the voice of the Holy Spirit within us, which is a privilege that all believers have. Any other way is an inferior form of covenantal living. Rules are a tragic substitute for the incredible dynamic of walking in the Spirit.

It is worth noting that Jesus did indeed raise the standard of the law during His earthly ministry, but it was certainly not for righteousness. He pointed out that men were not nearly as good at keeping the law as they thought they were, which was an enormous problem in the Jewish leadership of Christ's day. The Sermon on the Mount (Matthew 5-7) is a prime example of this, with Jesus using the law on his Jewish audience to show them how much they needed deliverance from it.

Those under the law would boast that they never broke the 7th Commandment, for they had not slept with another man's wife. Jesus stated that if you looked upon a woman and *wanted* to sleep with her, you were committing adultery in your heart (Matthew 5:27-28). He added murder to that list (5:21-22), as well as instructions regarding loving one's neighbor (5:43-44). These were not done to reinforce the law as the standard of God's holiness, but to bring His audience to the end of themselves so that they would cry out for their Redeemer. The Jews of His day were looking for a Messiah to save them from Rome, not one to save them from their inability to keep the law.

Ultimately, the purpose for Jesus living on earth as a man was to redeem mankind from the curse of the law, which ruled over him like a cruel taskmaster. Exhausted beneath the weight of performance-based righteousness, man was meant to turn to Christ as his Savior. He was offering the original promise of rest and inheritance to all who would come to Him. His gift to them would be righteousness and relationship, all accessible by faith. Just like Abraham believing God for righteousness, man could have the promise through believing in the Son.

Two Immutable Things

"That by two immutable things, in which it is impossible for God to lie, we might have strong consolation, who have fled for refuge to lay hold of the hope set before us." (Hebrews 6:18)

The "immutable" of Verse 18 points back to the "immutability" of Verse 17. The author spoke of "the immutability of His counsel," which we confirmed was "the unchangeableness of His purpose." The second point of Verse 17 was "confirmed by an oath," the sum total of these two gives us the "two immutable things."

Two unchangeable things, "in which it is impossible for God to lie." Two things which are rock-solid, so strong and so true that their existence affords us "strong consolation," make up the bulk of this verse, and provide us with a bed rock upon which God has established the Abrahamic Covenant. If we prove them to be unchangeable, then we are confident that God cannot lie, and we too can have strong consolation.

In a nutshell, the two immutable things are God's counsel and His oath. I cannot, and will not, try to convince you that God is unchangeable. I present the case as I see it, with scriptures in support; no one can truly convince another person of the unchangeableness of God's counsel and the power and effectiveness of His oath. I have seen too many instances where people hear the message of how good God is and their hearts nearly flutter in light of His favor, only to have someone "straighten them out," later. He is good and His Word confirms it. Can you accept it?

Look at God's unchangeable promise regarding His feelings under the New Covenant. Notice how He guarantees He will remember our sins and lawless deeds no more (Hebrews 10:17). See the blessedness of the man "to whom God imputes righteousness apart from works" (Romans 4:6). Watch as God, in light of the prophesied death of His Son in Isaiah 53, makes an almost unbelievable promise in Isaiah 54. I have marked the incredible promises in bold. See if you can believe them and accept them as God's immutable things (promises):

> *"For this is like the waters of Noah to Me; for as I have sworn that the waters of Noah would no longer cover the earth, so have I sworn that **I would not be angry with you, nor rebuke you.** For the mountains shall depart and the hills be removed, but **My kindness shall not depart from you, nor shall My covenant of peace be removed.**"* (Isaiah 54:9, 10)

The Hope Set Before Us

The immutable things provide us with a strong consolation in light of the fact that we have fled the things of this world "to lay hold of the hope set before us" (Hebrews 6:18). Paul said the hope was laid up for us in heaven (Colossians 1:5), confirming an internal security the believer has access to due to our faith that God cannot lie and will not change His mind.

> *"This hope we have as an anchor of the soul, both sure and steadfast, and which enters the Presence behind the veil, where the forerunner has entered for us, even Jesus, having become High Priest forever according to the order of Melchizedek."* (Hebrews 6:19, 20)

Our hope anchors our soul, which means that it provides stability of mind. It causes us to enter the Most Holy Place, beyond the veil of separation. No longer satisfied with access to the Holy Place, our newfound hope propels us into the room once forbidden to mere men like ourselves. Our forerunner, Christ Jesus, has made the way clear into the very Presence of God. The Ark of the Covenant, which once meant sure death to us because of our failures and our sins, now represents the very mercy we long for. Covered in the blood of countless sacrifices, the Ark had done us little good in securing our hope as an anchor. Now, covered in the blood of the One Sacrifice, we find rest and peace, in spite of ourselves.

Together, we are ready to journey backwards, to the time of Abraham, and to be eye-witnesses to one of history's watershed moments. If the cross represents the high-point of the New Testament, its historical companion surely represents the Old Testament's most important one. Our next chapter is the apex of this book. It is the reason for this writing, and its content is the reason for both the cross and the New Covenant. Let's head there together, armed with such valuable information about Calvary. Let's watch God cut a covenant, and see if we can find Christ in the shadows. Let's go between the pieces.

Chapter 10

Between the Pieces

T he covenant that God cut at Calvary was a unilateral one. It required no
assistance or participation from any other party. It excluded man from
the ceremony, yet included him in the benefits. Obviously, Jesus was
there, and was an active participant, but He was not a separate entity from the
Father. Exactly how Christ was involved is the source of some debate, as some
have Him as strictly the sacrifice, while others see Him as the party on the other
end of the bargaining table.

However one might view the cross in relation to the covenant, something is
undeniable, even if not understood: there was something covenantal happening
at the cross. Was that something a new thing, or the re-envisioning of an old
thing? Was God doing something He had never done before, or was He simply
replaying a previous event in an entirely new format?

These questions surface due to the fact that the New Covenant is so similar
in scope to the one God had with Abraham, and so opposite of the one He had
with Israel at Sinai. The more we focus on the Finished Work of Christ on the
cross, the more we see both the familiar and the brand new. Familiarity is evident
between the Father/Son paradigm and the Abraham/Isaac paradigm. Familiarity
is found in the darkness of the cross and the sleepy Abraham in Genesis 15.
A sacrifice is killed, literally split in half, when God cuts covenant with Abraham, promising to give to him what he cannot earn. The Lamb of God is killed,

severed if you will, when God cuts another covenant, promising the world – Gentiles included – what they too could never earn.

Something new was happening that fateful crucifixion day as well. God had never poured all of His anger out in one fell swoop, but He did at Calvary. God had never approved of human sacrifice, but He took the offering of His Son in full approval. No sacrifice had ever endured the fire and lived through the judgment, yet there is Jesus, on the other side of darkness, still alive and now ready to lay down His life willingly. God had never tasted death as a man, but on the cross He felt the full brunt of the human experience: pain, loss, betrayal, agony, loneliness, and a host of other emotions that no one can know without the twin peaks of both life and death.

Throughout the history of man, the cutting of covenant had been a ceremony rife with emotion, sacrifice and commitment. More than a contract, it was the lifeblood of peoples and nations. Sworn to allegiances through the cutting of covenant, men lived and died by the promises they made, and the scars they had incurred in order to establish trust and communion.

Most Bible students are aware of the covenant between David and Jonathan (1 Samuel 20:11-17). Though we will not examine the details of that covenant here, we should notice that it was necessary to "go out into the field," in order to cut the covenant. The text does not specify why they needed to do this, but any Hebrew who read the Torah would have known the reason, especially considering that Verse 16 says they "made a covenant."

Going to the open field was a necessity due to the complexity of the covenant ceremony. In a passage regarding a separate covenant King Zedekiah had made with the people of Jerusalem, we are given a vivid description of the actual cutting of covenant:

> *"And I will give the men who have transgressed My covenant, who have not performed the words of the covenant which they made before Me, when they cut the calf in two and passed between the parts of it – the princes of Judah, the princes of Jerusalem, the eunuchs, the priests, and all the people of the land who passed between the parts of the calf."* (Jeremiah 34:18, 19)

This description of the covenant ceremony includes the cutting of the sacrificial calf into two parts. These parts were divided – one on each side – and the covenantal parties passed between the parts of the animal. This passing between the animals was a physical act of committing to one another through oath, effectively swearing on the blood.

As we stated a few paragraphs ago, the covenant that God cut at Calvary was a unilateral one. Couple this with the fact that a covenant involves two parties and we have an obvious discrepancy. Now, factor in what we learned in the last few chapters about how God actually cut the Abrahamic Covenant in Christ. This means that God and Christ were somehow involved *together* in the cutting of covenant with Abraham, and that covenant was enhanced through the Finished Work of Christ. It's time to take a look at that original covenant and to learn how God could involve Christ, cut covenant with Abraham and have that covenant be unilateral all at the same time.

God's Covenant with Abraham

Genesis 15 contains one of the most important stories in the Bible. The entire Old Testament narrative hinges on its content, as God had lost His intimate communication with man through Adam's fall in Eden. Having called Abraham out of the land of his forefathers (Abraham was a Gentile at this time) in Genesis 12, God now begins the process of relationship with man through promise and oath. Ultimately the story will have a tragic twist, when Israel will prefer a change in covenant and go through centuries of pain due to their rejection of relationship. However at this early date, the picture of covenant given in Genesis 15 sets the pattern for how God really prefers to deal with man, and also gives us a glimpse at His ultimate plan: the cross of Christ.

> *"After these things the word of the LORD came to Abram in a vision, saying, 'Do not be afraid, Abram, I am your shield, your exceedingly great reward.' But Abram said, 'Lord GOD, what will You give me, seeing I go childless, and the heir of my house is Eliezer of Damascus?' Then Abram said, 'Look, You have given me no off-spring; indeed one born in my house is my heir!' And behold, the*

*word of the LORD came to him, saying, 'This one shall not be your
heir, but one who will come from your own body shall be your heir.'"*
(Genesis 15:1-4)

Abraham (at this point still named 'Abram') questions the Lord as to what the
exceeding great reward is going to be, though it is clear that the Lord considered
Himself that reward. Talk about a man showing doubt in the face of greatness!
Not content to have the Lord as his reward, Abraham extends the argument past
"What will you give me," to "You have given me no…" I read this text in awe at the
attitude of Abraham who, faced with a visitation of God, answers with a request
and an accusation. God's answer to such insolence is not fire from heaven or
some terrible disease, but another promise that Abraham will indeed have a son!

My old, religious side screams out "How dare you!" to both Abraham, and,
(dare I say it) to God. Surely God won't stand for such an attitude. Understanding why God puts up with this and continues to bless Abraham in spite of it, is to
understand the framework of grace.

God is intent on blessing the human family through faith. It was always His
intention and has always been His way. This story of Abraham is a microcosm
of God's insatiable desire to be good to undeserving man. At the cross we see the
most profound and demonstrative example of that favor and love. Together, the
story of God's dealing with Abraham, and the story of Christ's death at Calvary,
show us the original intent of heaven. Abraham deserves no favor, and yet he
receives it. Jesus deserves no judgment and yet He receives it. We identify with
both men; Abraham in that we are blessed and favored by faith; Christ in that He
has borne the punishment for our sins. In both cases, we win.

Written in the Stars

*"Then He brought him outside and said, 'Look now toward heaven,
and count the stars if you are able to number then.' And He said to
him, 'So shall your descendants be.'"* (Genesis 15:5)

God's instruction to Abram to "Look toward heaven, and count the stars," set a precedent for how Israel would come to view themselves. This is why Jacob responded the way he did to Joseph in Genesis 37 when Joseph told him of a dream in which the sun, the moon and the stars bowed down to him. Jacob declared, "What is this dream that you have dreamed? Shall your mother and I and your brothers indeed come to bow down to the earth before you?" (Genesis 37:10). Notice that when hearing about the sun, the moon and the stars, Jacob assumed it meant him and his family. That family would end up being called, "Israel."

The earth would be added to the description of Israel following Abraham's willingness to offer his son Isaac upon an altar as a sacrifice. God intervened, and provided Himself a goat, but in the accompanying blessing, He increased Abraham's revelation of covenant by promising to not only "multiply your descendants as the stars of the heaven," but also "as the sand which is on the seashore" (Genesis 22:17).

This establishment of Israel as "heaven and earth" was not to indicate that there was no such thing as a literal heavens or planet Earth, but rather to frame the narrative of the Scriptures. The volume of the book is written about Jesus (Hebrews 10:7), but the way in which He is presented is through the story of Israel and her system. When Israel was under the Mosaic Law we might call that system the "Mosaic Economy," but in essence it is the "heavens and the earth."

This explanation helps us interpret another saying of Jesus, which we covered in part in a previous chapter. Jesus declared that He did not come to destroy the law but to fulfill it. In the next verse in sequence, He speaks further of that fulfillment:

> *"For assuredly, I say to you, till heaven and earth pass away, not one jot or one tittle will by no means pass from the law till all is fulfilled."*
> (Matthew 5:18)

The jot and the tittle are the smallest letter and the smallest stroke in a Hebrew letter, respectively. Jesus promises that neither shall pass away from the law until all is fulfilled. What is often ignored (even in grace preaching) is the statement about heaven and earth passing away. The fulfillment of the law is kicked off with heaven and earth passing away. To us Gentiles, it seems to mean that the heavens we see in the sky and the earth we are standing on are going to pass away someday. What we miss is that Jesus told us that the law won't be completely fulfilled *until* heaven and earth pass away. This means that either the law is not fulfilled now (since we are still seeing the heavens and standing on the earth) or He meant something that every Jew easily understood.

Peter's sermon at Pentecost regarding Joel's last day prophecy promised the Spirit to be poured out on all flesh with sons and daughters prophesying and young and old men having visions and dreaming dreams. Unfortunately, we leave off the rest of Peter's sermon, but rest assured the Jews did not miss it!

> *"I will show wonders in heaven above and signs in the earth beneath: blood and fire and vapor of smoke. The sun shall be turned into darkness, and the moon into blood, before the coming of the great and awesome day of the LORD. And it shall come to pass that whoever calls on the name of the LORD shall be saved."* (Acts 2:19-21)

This part of the prophecy is the tail end of the "Pentecostal" portion we are so apt to quote. Peter declared all of it to be happening in front of their very eyes. My question is, when did the sun turn to darkness and the moon turn to blood? We can't just ignore that part on our way to the beautiful, all-inclusive promise that whoever calls on the name of the Lord will be saved.

Jews were perfectly aware of the imagery of the heavens and the earth as representative of their system of religion. For them, the darkening of the sun and the moon turning to blood was the end of an old way of doing things. It was "lights out," on the old Mosaic Economy. Calvary, and the covenant cut there, marked the end of an Old Covenant and the beginning of a whole new world. Slowly, but surely, the old system of sacrifices, priesthood and worshipping at a temple came to an end, and within one generation after Christ, it was gone forever.

It is also fascinating to note that the word used for "count" in Genesis 15:5 is also translated as "tell" in other passages of the Old Testament. God wasn't ordering Abram to tell something to the stars, but rather to see what the stars were telling him. This is not an advocacy for astrology, as that is man looking to the stars for instructions on how to live and what decisions to make. This early message written in the stars was God's natural phenomenon explaining the message of the good news. Much could be written – and much has been written – on the gospel story splayed across the heavens, but to simply whet your appetite, consider that from Virgo ("the virgin") to Leo ("the lion"), God is showing the story of His redemption plan through the man Christ Jesus. Abram was encouraged to read that message and to believe that out of that message his descendants were coming.

> "And he believed in the LORD and He accounted it to him for righteousness." (Genesis 15:6)

We dealt with the source of Abraham's righteousness two chapters ago so we won't dig too deep here. This verse is the backbone of our covenant, and one could say that an understanding of Genesis 15:6 is all that is necessary to a fundamental understanding of the New Covenant. Though the cutting of the New Covenant was centuries away from this moment, the foundation of what it stands for was birthed in this moment, when Abraham believed God and God decided that faith was what counted for righteousness. Any doctrine you adhere to that takes away from that beauty and simplicity should be re-evaluated and avoided.

Prove it!

> "Then He said to him, 'I am the LORD, who brought you out of Ur of the Chaldeans, to give you this land to inherit it.' And he said, 'Lord GOD, how shall I know that I will inherit it?'" (Genesis 15:7-8)

The admonition to count the stars was not enough proof to Abraham that God would be true to His promise. Though we know it was "immutable," He needed an oath on top of it for Abraham to feel secure.

For us, the cross is the physical sign of that promise, our proof of sorts. Calvary is the obvious physical manifestation of God's love for us. To understand the cross is to comprehend the love of God. To misunderstand the cross is to miss out on the greatest love story of them all. Paul called the cross the way that God demonstrates how much He loves us (Romans 5:8).

The Cutting of Covenant

"So He said to him, 'Bring Me a three-year-old heifer, a three-year-old female goat, a three-year-old ram, a turtledove, and a young pigeon.' Then he brought all these to Him and cut them in two, down the middle, and placed each piece opposite the other; but he did not cut the birds in two." (Genesis 15:9, 10)

I am hesitant to build too large a case around the numerology and the species involved in the cutting of this covenant. Some write with great authority on what each one represents, and the study is admittedly intriguing. However, much conjecture leads us into the deep waters of debate, and oftentimes there is more confusion when we are finished than when we started. There could be a glimpse of three covenantal periods in the three different, three-year-old species. Perhaps the Abrahamic (heifer – faith), the Mosaic (goat – law) and the New Covenants (ram – grace) are all typified. Maybe we see the ashes of a red heifer in Numbers 19 as the passing of one covenant to the next. It is possible that the Mosaic Law (goat) is what Jesus had in mind in His famous "goats on the left" speech of Matthew 25:31-34, and further, we could easily see the ram (grace) as being the one found in the thicket by Abraham on Mt. Moriah when God finally found a sacrifice for Himself.

While the previous ideas are worth investigating on their own, we can be certain that what was laid out by God in Genesis 15 regarding the sacrificial animals was a pre-cursor to His instructions for sacrifice in the Old Testament tabernacle (Leviticus 1:1-17). The difference found here and in the Mosaic instructions are in the gender of the animals and in their specific ages. Here, there is a heifer, while in the sacrificial system, it is a bullock. Also, God specifically tells Abraham to bring a female goat, while it should be a ram under the Mosaic Economy. As in the previous paragraph, conjecture may not be necessary.

No where else is there a specific command to use "three-year-old" animals. Rather than find a Hebrew meaning in the "three," it makes more practical sense to note that these particular animals are in the prime of their lives at three years old, having reached full maturity. A parallel to Christ could be that at Calvary, He too was in the prime of life.

The reasons for multiple options in regards to species had more to do with finance than spirituality. The wealthy were to bring the bullock; the poor man was to bring the more affordable pigeon and turtledove. Jesus' own family brought the latter when presenting Him to the temple, a sign that they were not wealthy. The spiritual implication could be that all people, great and small, rich and poor, are accounted for in the sacrifice. Just as God had Abram divide the heifer, the she-goat, the ram and the birds, there is enough covenant coverage for all classes, races and economic conditions.

One can imagine a great amount of blood was involved in the halving of so many animals. Abraham cut them in two and placed the pieces opposite one another with enough space between for two people to walk past. Traditionally, the two men involved in the oath would meet in the middle of animals and state their promises to one another, flanked by the sacrificial animals, and standing in blood. Everything is ready and Abraham sits back to await the arrival of God.

No Help Needed

"And when the vultures came down on the carcasses, Abram drove them away. Now when the sun was going down, a deep sleep fell upon Abram: and behold, horror and great darkness fell upon him." (Genesis 15:11-12)

As Abraham waited on God to appear, the smell of the dead animals filled the air, attracting the vultures that couldn't resist such an easy meal. Wanting to be sure and preserve the sacrifices he had worked so hard to prepare, Abraham drove the birds away, protecting the ground for covenant. As the sun went down, Abraham experienced a fatigue that was due to more than the weariness of a long day. Scripture is quick to include that a "horror and great darkness fell upon him." Abraham wasn't *falling* asleep he was being *put* to sleep.

I don't want to be too hard on Abraham, but due to the fact that God is about to cut this covenant without Abraham's involvement, and the Scripture specifically states that great darkness fell upon him, we can conclude that God saw Abraham's chasing of the vultures as his attempt to be involved in the covenant.

Perhaps the deep sleep was going to occur anyway, but the very presence of the "vulture verse" tells us that it was a moment of significance. Abraham's protection of the sacrifice might indeed be a noble work (he is neither punished nor reprimanded for it), but it also speaks to man's incessant need to involve himself in his own redemption.

Granted, Abraham gathered the animals, cut them in half, set up the covenant ceremony, and fully expected to be an active participant, but did not realize that the actual covenant could not involve him, lest he be held responsible for his end of the oath. Any participation by Abraham during the actual cutting of covenant could constitute him being bound to obligation. Whatever he was obligated to do would then be his responsibility and God would be forced by the terms of the covenant to bless him or curse him accordingly.

A scriptural connection that should not be overlooked is found in Genesis 2:21 when God put Adam in a deep sleep in order to form woman from his side. From a place of rest, Adam gets his Eve. From a place of rest, Abraham gets his covenant. From a place of rest, Jacob sees into heaven (Genesis 28:11). From a place of rest, we receive the benefits of Christ's Finished Work.

The place of rest is so vital because it precludes our involvement. As long as we are actively involved in our victory or our transformation, we are not resting in the fact that Jesus finished the work *on our behalf*. I emphasize that last phrase because we should never forget that Jesus did not need to finish a work on His own behalf, for He had no sin and had no problem with victory. Whatever He accomplished (and it is your honor to uncover those accomplishments), He did it for us!

The Prophecy and the Promise

"Then He said to Abram: 'Know certainly that your descendants will be strangers in a land that is not theirs, and will serve them, and they will afflict them four hundred years. And also the nation whom they serve I will judge; afterward they shall come out with great possessions. Now as for you, you shall go to your fathers in peace; you shall be buried at a good old age. But in the fourth generation they

shall return here, for the iniquity of the Amorites is not yet complete."
(Genesis 15:13-16)

During Abraham's deep sleep, the Lord spoke to him, probably through a dream. The message relayed sets us up for the Exodus experience, when God's people are strangers in the land of Egypt. Couple the promise of "four hundred years" with Paul's statement about the giving of the law and we learn something about the timing:

> *"And this I say, that the law, which was four hundred and thirty years later, cannot annul the covenant that was confirmed before by God in Christ, that it should make the promise of no effect."* (Galatians 3:17)

God speaks of Israel being strangers, and afflicted, for four hundred years while Paul states that the law – given at Mt. Sinai to Moses – came four hundred and thirty years after the promise to Abraham. There is no discrepancy here as the clock is starting at two different points in each verse. In God's promise to Abraham, He states "your descendants will be strangers…four hundred years." That starts the four hundred year clock with the descendents of Abraham, which would specifically be Isaac. Isaac was not yet born at the time of the promise, which accounts for the missing thirty years.

Since Paul states that the law given to Moses came four hundred and thirty years after the Abrahamic Covenant, it is not possible that the children of Israel were enslaved in Egypt for four hundred years like many of us have believed. However, God views the entire journey from the promise to Abraham into the Promised Land as one of afflicted strangers. Until Israel arrived in her promised land of rest, she was not everything she was destined to be.

God fulfilled His promise of Verse 14 when He judged Egypt through the plagues and at the waters of the Red Sea. Israel also came out of the land "with great possessions" (Psalm 105:37). His promise of Verse 15 belonged strictly to Abraham, and was fulfilled when Abraham died at age 175.

Finally, the promise that a "fourth generation" would return to that spot included the reasoning of "the iniquity of the Amorites is not yet complete." The length of a generation has differed at different periods of time throughout history. The indication here is that it was somewhere around one hundred years, meaning that after the four hundred years prophesied, Israel would return to the land that Abraham was standing on. In later times, the generation length seems to have dropped to between thirty and forty years (Job 42:16).

Apparently the journey of Israel into the Promised Land would include the punishment of the Amorites for centuries of rebellion. We can read too much into this phrase quite easily, which would include ideas about God presenting Himself to the Amorites and them rejecting Him, but we end in much conjecture. It is evident that God had judgment in mind for the Amorites (which included all people occupying the land of Canaan).

Between the Pieces

Everything in the story of Abraham's covenant has been building up to this point. The very book you're reading has been leading up to this moment from the outset, with us finally arriving at the title segment. The path is laid out, the animals have been killed and the blood has been shed. Abraham is asleep and resting in God's promises, and now there is nothing left to do but show up and cut covenant.

Abraham was a mere man, full of flaws and imperfections. For God to enter into covenant with him would have had disastrous results. To establish an entire nation out of one man, it was necessary to have mercy available to that man. To judge him with curses and possibly death was to cut off the possibility of future generations. Expansion was only possible through a covenant of grace, just like the technological and mental expansion of the human race has been made possible through the grace of God allowing men the process of trial and error.

In the modern church's seeming fascination with a return to a theocratic system of both national and self-government, it is often overlooked as to how limited and backward we would be if such a system came to pass. The law forbade the touching of dead bodies without ceremonial washing and cleansing. Our advancements in medical science would not have been possible under such a system.

A male doctor was limited in how he could treat a female patient since many things were deemed inappropriate. Some diseases would go undetected and untreated without God's grace.

Women were given no option for divorce under the law. If they were in a relationship with a violent, cheating husband, they were to consider it their lot in life and submit willingly. Only God's grace afforded them the possibility of a better life; the law did not.

We could nitpick and find many more (the law nitpicked, so why not?). Men could marry multiple wives. Slavery was considered a way of life. Teenage rebellion warranted capital punishment and a woman could be put through a detailed ritual of cleansing just because her husband thought she was cheating. You couldn't wear two different kinds of fabric on your body at the same time (there goes cotton underwear beneath denim) and advances in indoor plumbing would never have happened, because you did your business in a hole in the ground outside the camp...and you dug the hole! (Deuteronomy 23:12-13)

I am not sharing these things to make the law look bad, for as Paul stated, it was just, holy and good (Romans 7:12). However, the law was deceiving in that men thought it could provide them with life, but it actually brought death (Romans 7:10). The fundamental reason behind this was that the law was built on a covenant between God and Israel in which Israel had to keep their end of the covenant or they were cursed. In other words, death was an automatic side effect!

This simply would not do in the establishment of a kingdom. God needed to remove Abraham from the equation, so He put Him to sleep. However, how does God establish an oath with Abraham without including him in the ceremony? That brings us back to the oath scripture from Hebrews:

"For when God made a promise to Abraham, because He could swear by no one greater, He swore by Himself." (Hebrews 6:13)

This speaks to more than the fact that God swore so that we would believe. God had no one to cut covenant with (Abraham is asleep!) so He "swore by Himself."

"And it came to pass, when the sun went down and it was dark, that behold, there appeared a smoking oven and a burning torch that passed between those pieces." (Genesis 15:17)

In the darkness, while Abraham slept nearby, a smoking oven and a burning torch passed between the pieces of sacrificial animal. This passing constituted an oath being made, with Hebrews assuring us that it was God swearing by Himself. Let's keep it simple and see what the early church would have seen based upon what they knew about God.

The Smoking Oven

"Therefore, since we are receiving a kingdom which cannot be shaken, let us have grace, by which we may serve God acceptably with reverence and godly fear. For our God is a consuming fire." (Hebrews 12:28-29)

Just as God was building a new kingdom through the Abrahamic Covenant, we have a kingdom built on grace. Only through His grace do we have an acceptable reverence and godly fear as reverence and fear under law should now be considered *unacceptable*. Our God is a consuming fire, and not placing Him in proper perspective is dangerous.

The Hebrews knew this God of fire (which is almost always purifying, not judgmental). Their first image of God was similar, as His glory was bright, like a purifying fire:

"The sight of the glory of the LORD was like a consuming fire on the top of the mountain in the eyes of the children of Israel." (Exodus 24:17)

Moses made a distinction between God's voice coming from heaven and the manifestation of His glory on this earth as through the fire:

"Out of heaven He let you hear His voice, that He might instruct you; on earth He showed you His great fire, and you heard His words out of the midst of the fire." (Deuteronomy 4:36)

At the end of the Old Testament, the prophet Malachi takes the imagery from the Abrahamic Covenant and applies it to the Lord:

*"For behold, the day is coming, **burning like an oven**, and all the proud, yes, all who do wickedly will be stubble. And the day which is coming shall burn them up,' says the LORD of hosts."* (Malachi 4:1)

In that same chapter, Malachi then tells of the coming of Elijah before that great day (Malachi 4:5). Jesus identified that Elijah as John the Baptist (Matthew 17:11-13). When John the Baptist comes on the scene, he picks up Malachi's illustration of the burning oven and takes it a step further:

"I indeed baptize you with water unto repentance, but He who is coming after me is mightier than I, whose sandals I am not worthy to carry, He will baptize you with the Holy Spirit and fire. His winnowing fan is in His hand, and He will thoroughly clean out His threshing floor, and gather his wheat into the barn; but He will burn up the chaff with unquenchable fire." (Matthew 3:11-12)

The burning of the chaff took place in a smoking oven of God's fire. That same smoking oven passed between the pieces in covenantal promise. See the oven as the nature of God.

Since God swore by Himself, and we know He was the smoking oven, how do we account for the burning torch? Is the torch simply another example of who God is and what He does? Or, could the torch be something else?

The Burning Torch

*"In Him was life, and the life was **the light** of men."* (John 1:4)

*"That was the true **Light** which gives light to every man coming into the world".* (John 1:9)

*"Then Jesus spoke to them again, saying, '**I am the light** of the world. He who follows Me shall not walk in darkness, but have the light of life."* (John 8:12)

*"As long as I am in the world, **I am the light** of the world."* (John 9:5)

*"The city had no need of the sun or of the moon to shine in it, for the glory of God illuminated it. **The Lamb is its light.**"* (Revelation 21:23)

The light in these scriptures is Jesus, also called "the Lamb." It's the same light that appeared to Saul on the road to Damascus, changing him forever into Paul, the apostle to the Gentiles. That same light in Paul sprang up, just as prophesied, as "A light to bring revelation to the Gentiles, and the glory of Your people Israel" (Luke 2:32).

The Father and the Son are one (John 10:30), and cannot be separated, for the Father never leaves the Son alone (John 8:29). But the two certainly have distinct works. Jesus strived to do the will of the Father, and His death on Calvary was the ultimate sign of obedience to what the Father desired. While God is as much "the Light" as is Jesus, the distinction should be noted as to how often the New Testament specifically refers to Jesus as the light, with Jesus Himself using the metaphor.

When God cut the Abrahamic Covenant, the smoking oven (God the Father) and the burning lamp (God the Son – Christ) passed between the pieces of the animal. Rather than to include fallen Abraham, God swore by Himself, introducing Christ into the ceremony. By cutting covenant with Himself, God could be held responsible for both ends of the covenant relationship. The oven and the lamp would forever characterize the passing between the pieces by Father and Son, linking them in an everlasting oath to bless the sleeping man based solely upon his faith.

This explains what Paul comprehended in his letter to the Galatians that God would confirm the covenant "in Christ" (Galatians 4:17). Calvary would be a re-telling of the Abrahamic Covenant. Christ was indeed involved the first time, as the burning lamp, and Jesus (the Christ) was involved in the New Covenant as that same burning lamp, or better, "the Light of the world."

The Darkness at Calvary

The darkness at Calvary was due to the obscuring of the sun (Luke 23:45), but that does little to explain what was *happening*. As we explained in an earlier chapter, we should refrain from viewing that moment as the forsaking of Jesus by His Father. Instead, let us connect the cutting of covenant in Genesis 15 with the cutting of covenant at Calvary.

The Father and Son passed between the pieces in one covenant, and thus, they did the same thing in the New Covenant. The darkness at the cross could be spiritualized as that moment when God and Jesus passed one another in covenant. Like the space between two people walking away from one another, the cosmos went dark when the unified Father and Son sealed the deal in blood. This darkness is the area behind God's back, (Isaiah 38:17), where Jesus suffered and died. Our redemption was bought and paid for in that moment, in that passing, in that space, where the light of the world suffered beneath the furnace of heaven. See it again through new eyes:

> "Surely He has borne our griefs and carried our sorrows; yet we esteemed Him stricken, smitten by God, and afflicted. But He was wounded for our transgressions, He was bruised for our iniquities; the chastisement for our peace was upon Him, and by His stripes we are healed." (Isaiah 53:4-5)

The darkness secured our salvation because it guaranteed that nothing gets lost behind God's back. No matter how rough life becomes, or how lonely we might feel, we can know that Jesus has already experienced the coldness behind God's back so that we can live every moment in the light of love. He has suffered in the dark so we could succeed in the light!

The Similarities

At Abraham's Covenant, he slept while God worked. Oblivious to what was happening only feet away, Abraham missed the mighty implications of God swearing an oath with Himself. At what point the next day did he realize what had happened?

At the cross, the crowd was in a spiritual slumber while God was working. The rulers of Israel, the Roman soldiers, and the gathered throng were oblivious to what was happening on a cross only a few feet away. The crowd missed the eternal implications of God cutting a New Covenant with Himself. At what point do we awake and realize what has happened?

Though Abraham was ignorant of the happenings between the pieces, what was happening there was happening on his behalf. He was the direct recipient of all that occurred in that dark, bloody moment. From that moment forward, only his faith was needed to afford him all the promises of that awesome oath.

Though we are often ignorant of the mighty importance of the Father and the Son passing between the pieces at Calvary, all of it was happening on our behalf. We are the direct recipient of all that occurred in that dark and bloody moment. From then onward, God has forgotten our sins and iniquities and has declared us forever righteous on the basis of our faith. That faith ensures us a full co-inheritance with Christ, and all spiritual blessings (Ephesians 1:3).

Abraham left that scene without a full revelation of what had just occurred. In the next chapter, as if God never promised him a son of his own through promise, Abraham sleeps with his wife's maid and bears a son of the flesh, Ishmael. Several years later God appears to Abraham and blesses him with that son of promise: Isaac. Abraham had not improved in his character, but God was blessing him anyhow.

We leave the scene of the cross without a full revelation of what has occurred on our behalf. In the subsequent chapters of our lives we live, at times, as if we have forgotten all about God's mighty promises and we cheat ourselves by linking up with the things of this world. We sow seeds of discord and works and end up with their by-products: guilt, condemnation, hatred, envying, strife, etc. Several years later, still passionately in love with us, God somehow breaks through our haze and blesses us in spite of ourselves. We may not have improved our character, but God keeps blessing us anyhow.

There is no way to account for these occurrences, both in Abraham and in us, other than to realize the overwhelming power of the covenant. These comparisons are not meant to instill a sense of irresponsibility regarding our walk with God, but to give us an assurance of the power of the cross. It is why Paul, when addressing the varied and remarkable needs of his church at Corinth, opened with his purpose: "For I determined not to know anything among you except Jesus Christ and Him crucified" (1 Corinthians 2:2). His determination was not to just repeat the events of the crucifixion over and over again, but to declare the covenant that was cut on that day.

Communion Declares Covenant

There were three important things that were to occur as part of the oath of covenant. There was an animal to be sacrificed; gifts were to be exchanged; and a meal was to be shared. I have often wondered if Abraham struggled with the comprehension of covenant early on because of his failure to commune with God through a shared meal.

The first two requirements were dealt with. The heifer, goat, ram and birds were offered as sacrifices, fulfilling the first important point and God gave Abraham the twin gifts of prophecy and promise to fulfill the second. However, there is no covenant meal exchanged. Surely it should have been done so, as even the elders of Israel ate in the presence of God at Mount Sinai in Exodus 24:11.

To link Abraham with the covenant forever, God visits him again in Genesis 18. On this visit, Abraham is quick to order a covenant meal to be shared under the shade of some trees. This meeting brings a promise to Abraham and Sarah regarding the soon birth of Isaac, and it prompts a spirit of intercession on the part of Abraham in defense of the people of Sodom against pending judgment. The sharing of the meal seems to give a heightened sense of revelation on the part of Abraham as to what is his under the covenant provisions.

Comparatively, the New Covenant contains the three important elements of the oath as well. Jesus was the Lamb of God that died to take away the sin of the world, fulfilling the need for a sacrifice. His advent, life, death and resurrection have brought myriad gifts to the human family, not the least of which is His awesome grace. Paul described us as having been "given according to the measure of Christ's gift," and that He "gave gifts to men" (Ephesians 4:7, 8).

Obviously, we are missing the third element of covenant: the meal. On the night before His crucifixion, Jesus shared the bread and the wine with His disciples, and His words of intensity speak louder about His heart than anything we could add:

> *"Then He said to them, 'With fervent desire I have desired to eat this Passover with you before I suffer."* (Luke 22:15)

As we discussed in Chapter 6, the Greek wording helps us to better understand Jesus' passion. The word that we translate "desire" is from the Greek word "epithumia" and it is better translated "lust." Jesus is stating that He has a fervent lust, and He has lusted to eat the Passover meal with His disciples. What could drive Him to use such language, and to feel so passionately about it, if not the knowledge that the sharing of a communion meal opens our eyes to the provisions of that covenant?

He broke the bread and called it His body. He shared the wine and called it His blood. "This is My body which is given for you: do this in remembrance of Me," (Luke 22:19) and "This cup is the new covenant in My blood, which is shed for you" (Luke 22:20). The sharing of that meal, and His encouragement for us to do the same while remembering Him, is our link to covenant provisions.

When we partake of the body of Jesus we are identifying with the life-giving qualities of His Finished Work. We are seeing all of our sicknesses and diseases as having been paid for in His sacrifice, and we are eating to ourselves His health and wholeness. This is not magical or superstitious; it is covenant!

The wine represents the blood of the New Covenant, pointing us to that bloody ground where Father and Son passed between the pieces. Our sins have been atoned for beneath that blood, for someone has already died there, for us. We function under a covenant of faith rather than performance. We have better promises and a better covenant all because a better Man did the work for us.

"For if by the one man's offense many died, much more the grace of God and the gift by the grace of the one Man, Jesus Christ, abounded to many." (Romans 5:15)

Dark No More

The sun has come up and a new day has dawned. All of our failures and our insufficiencies have been atoned for through the darkness of a place called Calvary. Just as Abraham stood up and went on his way following the night of deep slumber, so we arise and go forth into a world of new horizons and new possibilities.

"For you were once darkness, but now you are light in the Lord. Walk as children of light." (Ephesians 5:8)

Jesus has suffered the darkness and has birthed us into the light of the Lord. We now walk, not as slaves to our dark past, but as children who can see clearly for the first time. We know that we haven't arrived at a full revelation of what we will be, but we won't be fooled again into thinking that God is judging us on the basis of our works and our effort.

"Brethren, I do not count myself to have apprehended; but one thing I do, forgetting those things which are behind and reaching forward to those things which are ahead, I press toward the goal for the prize of the upward call of God in Christ Jesus." (Philippians 3:13-14)

"Forget the things which are behind." What glorious advice! Behind God's back there is no room to dwell. Christ has suffered there and we are free from the abandonment and condemnation of our past. Ahead of us is the light of God, which is always shining on our righteousness in Christ. As a great songwriter once said, "Tomorrow may rain, so I'll follow the sun."[1]

"Therefore He says: 'Awake, you who sleep, arise from the dead, and Christ will give you light.'" (Ephesians 5:14)

Endnote

1. Lennon-McCartney, *I'll Follow the Sun*, from *Beatles For Sale*, EMI, Parlophone, Capitol, 1964

Chapter 11

Everlasting Covenant; Everlasting Consolation

L et's start this chapter with some thoughts about the Abrahamic Covenant, the Mosaic Covenant (Old Covenant) and the New Covenant.

> *"And I will establish My covenant between Me and you and your descendants after you in their generations, for an everlasting covenant, to be God to you and your descendants after you."* (Genesis 17:7)

The concept of an everlasting covenant did not originate with the New Covenant cut at Calvary. All covenants were to remain effective until one party died. The everlasting quality of the New Covenant is found in the fact that both sides are eternal. Neither the Father nor the Son will be going anywhere!

Since the Abrahamic Covenant was cut while Abraham slept, eliminating him from the obligation of upholding covenant, it also removed his death as the endpoint of the covenant. It was God passing between the sacrificial pieces, cutting covenant with Himself, which guaranteed an everlasting quality that most assuredly still stands.

Paul explained to the Galatians that the Mosaic Covenant given on Mt. Sinai could not annul the Abrahamic Covenant, meaning that the law *did not* remove the everlasting covenant promised to Abraham. The confirmation of the Abrahamic Covenant to an entirely new generation was the cross of Christ, where God let the entire world see in vivid detail what He had always wanted to accomplish. The cross actually doubled as confirmation for the Abrahamic Covenant and as the starting point for what we live under: the New Covenant.

The parallels of the Abrahamic Covenant and the New Covenant are best explained by identifying the "Seed" to whom the promises of the Abrahamic Covenant were made (that Seed is Jesus). In doing this, Paul made the provisions of that covenant as eternal as Christ Himself. For those who place their faith in Christ, they too become "Abraham's seed," and are then recipients of Abraham's promise (Galatians 3:29).

The Old Covenant was based upon works, and God was bound to curse the people who broke their end of the oath. As we discussed in a previous chapter, God eventually gave the people what they wanted and He broke the Old Covenant for them. Their purchase price in buying Him off was thirty pieces of silver, brought from prophecy to reality through the betrayal of Jesus by Judas Iscariot.

Jesus' death on the cross was the confirmation of the Abrahamic Covenant, the cutting of a New Covenant and the death of one half of the Old Covenant (since Jesus was the representative man of the Old Covenant). This brought Abraham's promise full circle, finished off the obligations of the Old Mosaic Covenant and established a new way of dealing with humanity. The finished work of Christ on the cross was obviously a "finish" in more ways than one, while also establishing a brand new beginning.

From Calvary through the end of the Mosaic Economy, which finally concluded for good with the fall of the temple and the priesthood during the Roman invasion of Jerusalem in AD 70, the vestiges of the Old Covenant were slowly fading away. This prompted the author of Hebrews to say, "He has made the first obsolete. Now what is becoming obsolete and growing old is ready to vanish away" (Hebrews 8:13). It was the Old Covenant that was growing old and was very soon gone for good.

I establish this point so that we can have proper understanding of which covenant is being referred to when we see the New Testament version of an everlasting covenant:

"Now may the God of peace who brought up our Lord Jesus from the dead, that great Shepherd of the sheep, through the blood of the everlasting covenant, make you complete in every good work...." (Hebrews 13:20, 21)

Compare the above verse with Genesis 17:7, which we used at the top of this chapter. Both speak of an "everlasting covenant." The first is regarding the covenant between God and Abraham and his descendants. The second is referencing a covenant cut "through the blood," designed to "make you complete." This means that the New Covenant is not only endless and everlasting, but it is ever working. It is not a dry, stale contract between Father and Son which exists only in theological terms. It is a vibrant, alive, life-changing oath in which God promises to transform man through the shed blood of the sacrifice.

This promise of change, in which we are made complete to perform every good work, does not ride on the back of our performance. It is simply a by-product of God having raised Jesus from the dead after His blood was shed for our sins. We identify with His death and then accept His life in us. He goes to work in us, preparing us to do works in the natural.

We will go deeper into the identification of His death in our final chapter, but first, let's look at the fulcrum of our New Covenant understanding. The book of Hebrews calls God, "the God of peace." A revelation of this one little description could serve as the key to unlocking great things in our covenant comprehension.

The God of Peace

The concept of a God of peace is foreign to the Old Testament. That is not to say that there was no peace in God throughout its pages, but that it is not the idea of God that is derived when one reads it. In fact, the phrase "God of peace" is never found from Genesis to Malachi. The closest we get is in Isaiah 9:6, when the coming Messiah is described as "everlasting Father and Prince of Peace." Notice that reference is actually about *Jesus,* who is the central figure of the New Covenant.

Once the cross accomplished the judgment against sin, and the resurrection assured that life wins, the New Testament comes alive with references of a God of peace. Directly, and word-for-word, the phrase appears five times. We have already read the one from Hebrews 13:20. Let's look at the other four:

"Now the God of peace be with you all. Amen." (Romans 15:33)

"And the God of peace will crush Satan under your feet shortly. The grace of our Lord Jesus Christ be with you. Amen." (Romans 16:20)

"The things which you learned and received and heard and saw in me, these do, and the God of peace will be with you." (Philippians 4:9)

"Now may the God of peace Himself sanctify you completely; and may your whole spirit, soul, and body be preserved blameless at the coming of our Lord Jesus Christ." (2 Thessalonians 5:23)

These references show us that God is identified with peace in our daily walk (Romans 15:33), in victory over the enemy (Romans 16:20), in wisdom and revelation (Philippians 4:9), in sanctification (2 Thessalonians 5:23) and in our future development (Hebrews 13:20). In short, the early church saw God as being at peace in every aspect of Christian experience.

These were simply the exact renderings of "God of peace," but they are not the only references to this remarkable aspect of a decidedly New Covenant God:

- The angels that declared the arrival of Baby Jesus said to the shepherds abiding in the fields, "Glory to God in the highest, and on earth peace, goodwill toward men!" (Luke 2:14).

- Jesus declared "Peace be with you," to a frightful group of disciples on Resurrection evening. When that introduction failed to bring them peace, He showed them the wounds in His hands and His side, giving them a revelation of the Finished Work. This made them glad, and ready for His refrain of "Peace to you!" (John 20:19-21).

- To the Jewish nation, ravished by centuries of war and subjugation by invaders, whose mindset was established on the idea that God was perpetually angry, and whose consciousness was warped by the persistent shedding of sacrificial blood, Peter spoke a new message:

> *"The word which God sent to the children of Israel, preaching peace through Jesus Christ – He is Lord of all".* (Acts 10:36)

- Paul's entire message of justification by faith was built upon the idea that God is no longer at war with mankind and is no longer angry at the transgressions accrued under an Old Covenant. Our entrance into the New Covenant of grace happens by our faith in Jesus Christ, which mirrors the faith in God that Abraham exhibited to enter into covenant. In Romans 5:1, Paul says, "Therefore, having been justified by faith, we have peace with God through our Lord Jesus Christ." Our peace with God is through Jesus Christ, since it was Christ who offered Himself as the sacrificial lamb at Calvary.

However the cross of Jesus Christ appears in the eyes of God is directly parallel to how at peace He is with us. Since the cross was not done on Christ's behalf, but on our behalf, what it affected was our standing with God. If God is at peace as long as the sacrifice of the cross appeases Him, then we are safe for that amount of time, and no longer. In other words, the only thing you need to worry about is whether or not Jesus messes up!

Actually, trying to frame the New Covenant by the clock is a little like trying to empty the ocean with a teaspoon. We try to grasp the eternal concepts of God's grace and we end up with words like "infinity" and "forever," but even in those we are limiting the beauty of His everlasting qualities.

Everlasting Life

Hebrews 13:20 tells us of an "everlasting covenant," which we know to be the New Covenant. However, as we pointed out a few paragraphs ago, Genesis 17:7 speaks of an "everlasting covenant" as well. While the Genesis covenant is Abraham's and the Hebrews covenant is ours, they are both represented in the cross, solving the mystery as to how both can be "everlasting."

That does not, however, solve another problem, which is posed in reference to the Mosaic Covenant. Isaiah 24:5 describes the Old Covenant as "the everlasting covenant." How can the Old Covenant be "everlasting" if it doesn't last forever? We know the law was a temporary measure, meant to force man to acknowledge his own inabilities and to cry out for a redeemer, but how do we get around the fact that it was supposed to be "everlasting?"

There is no need to "get around" anything. We must simply learn to interpret scripture based upon its context. The Hebrew word often translated "everlasting" or "forever" is "olam." In Psalm 118:29, "His mercy endures forever," the word "forever" is "olam," which obviously indicates a mercy that lasts through infinity. However, the same word is used by Jonah, to describe how long he was trapped in the belly of the whale. "The earth with its bars closed behind me forever" (Jonah 2:6). Jonah was obviously mistaken, as Jonah 1:17 tells us that he was in the belly of the fish three days and three nights. Why would he use a word (olam) that often translates to "forever," to describe something that he knew did not last forever? (It is important to note that Jonah is writing of how he viewed the experience, after the fact, which means he used that word on purpose.)

I'm not trying to stir controversy, or lead you off on a separate study of word usage. I am merely setting us up for a beautiful quality of the New Covenant that goes beyond it simply lasting "forever."

The New Testament Greek equivalent of the Old Testament Hebrew word "olam" is the word "aion." Just as we saw in the Old Testament, the usage and context of the word determines its interpretation (regardless of how the translators handled it – or mishandled it!). One verse in particular gives us the same Greek word three times, and produces three *different* English words to describe it:

> "Now to the King eternal (aion), immortal, invisible, to God who alone is wise, be honor and glory forever (aion) and ever (aion). Amen." (1 Timothy 1:17)

Sometimes, like in Matthew 24:3, the word "aion" is a time-bound word. The disciples want to know when will be the "end of the age?" The word "age" is "aion." They surely aren't asking, "When will be the end of forever" for that would make no sense, thus the translators correctly took the same Greek word and framed it within time (though the KJV incorrectly translates it "world").

The Greek word "aion" is the root word for most of the uses of "everlasting" in the New Testament. In most Greek lexicons, the word will appear as "aionios," but they are both displaying the same intent.

Perhaps one of the most famous uses of "aion" could also be one of the most misunderstood. Jesus makes a declaration and a promise when speaking to Nicodemus regarding the born-again experience.

"For God so loved the world that He gave His only begotten Son, that whoever believes in Him should not perish but have everlasting (aionios) life." (John 3:16)

Most of us read John 3:16 and assume that Jesus is promising life that never ends to those who believe in Him. Yet, the contrast that Jesus draws is not between someone having endless punishment versus someone having endless pleasure. Jesus indicates that all are presently living a life to perish, but faith in the only begotten Son (Jesus), guarantees the life of the everlasting. This shouldn't be framed by time, for it cheapens the gift. This verse is a promise that when one receives Christ, he can walk in the light of a higher life. He can truly have the life of the Kingdom!

Using that same framework, consider the power of an everlasting covenant. This is not necessarily a reference to a covenant that lasts forever as much as it is to one that holds the qualities of an endless dimension. The New Covenant is unlike anything in the temporal, tangible world, thus it is everlasting. To say that its everlasting quality means it goes on forever – though it certainly does go on forever – misses the most important point: the New Covenant holds the everlasting qualities of its Creator. As God's very character and nature bears out, this Covenant is just like Him!

When one walks in the realities of the New Covenant, he is walking in the knowledge that his redemptive work is finished. There is no covenant in effect that involves his performance and his works. He is walking – and resting – in Christ's finished work and what He accomplished through the covenantal cutting of Calvary. To base our anointing, blessing, favor, fellowship or proximity to God upon anything other than the cutting of Christ's covenant is to insert ourselves into the covenant cut between God and His Son. This is a subtle – and sometimes blatant – attempt to elevate the Old Covenant to the same status as the

New. It is both insulting and damaging, and it lessens the shine on the everlasting qualities of the cross and the empty tomb.

Everlasting Consolation

> *"Now may our Lord Jesus Christ Himself, and our God and Father, who has loved us and given us everlasting consolation and good hope by grace, comfort your hearts and establish you in every good word and work."* (2 Thessalonians 2:16, 17)

Because of the Lord Jesus Christ, and the love that has been displayed to us through His sacrificial death, each of us have been given everlasting consolation. This consolation is not earned because it is specifically referred to as a gift. God wants you to know that you can rest in the consolation of the everlasting realm. Also, contextually, it is not a stretch to say that the "aionios" here does indeed speak of something being eternal in our realm. You can be just as confident and secure in your salvation as God is in the finished work of His Son.

The word "consolation" is translated as "the comfort of the Holy Ghost" in Acts 9:31 and as "exhortation" in Romans 12:8. Through Christ we have an everlasting comfort and exhortation. By connecting Christ to our consolation, Paul is telling the church that what Jesus accomplished at Calvary was enough for them to rest secure in this New Covenant. John spoke of this endless quality in a different way:

> *"But if we walk in the light as He is in the light, we have fellowship with one another, and the blood of Jesus Christ His Son cleanses us from all sin."* (1 John 1:7)

John isn't putting conditions on our cleansing; he is just comparing two ways to walk. One can walk in darkness or walk in light. In darkness there is no cleansing, but in the light He cleanses us from all sin. The Greek tense of the verb "cleanses" indicates an ongoing action, meaning the blood of Jesus is ALWAYS cleansing us from our sins!

Please notice the necessary connection between an everlasting covenant and an everlasting consolation. If the covenant that we function under is dependent upon our performance, it does not retain the qualities of the Everlasting One. Jesus "ever lives to make intercession" (Hebrews 7:25), and His endless life shows us the longevity and depth of the New Covenant. Since the covenant that we rest in is essentially between Father and Son, and we are recipients of the benefits by faith, we are living in an everlasting covenant. Without that knowledge, our consolation would be built upon our performance, rather than Christ's finished work.

For many of us, our Christian experience has been full of shaky consolation at best. We gave our hearts to Christ under the pretense that Jesus paid it all and we could accept His grace gift of salvation simply by confession and repentance. After our conversion, the "fine print" segment of our Christianity kicked in and we learned how much we needed to do in order to maintain our salvation. God was painted as perpetually angry at sin while Jesus was the tender voice calming the Father down after we had confessed and repented again. The Holy Spirit was around to tell us what to do and to put us under heavy conviction when we didn't do the right thing.

The preceding definition of Christianity has led some people to contact my ministry and state that the day they got saved was one of the most regrettable moments of their life! I can only imagine the state of desperation one must arrive at to even articulate his feelings in such a manner, and I sympathize. It's not that people have "fallen out of love" with Jesus, but that they came to Him for freedom from the burdens they carried, only to have another yoke placed upon them of works and performance that they were completely incapable of carrying.

Let it be known now and forever, *the Holy Spirit was not placed inside of you to help you keep the law.* Jesus has already kept the law, and God isn't waiting on someone else to perform for Him! You are now alive in Christ Jesus so that His life can show forth out of you. The Holy Spirit simply glorifies Jesus in us. What was external under the Mosaic Covenant (laws, ordinances and commands) is now internal under the New Covenant. His Spirit leads and guides you into all truth, and as you learn to follow Him by your spiritual senses, you are indeed led into a life of good works (Hebrews 5:14).

Once you let that revelation sink into your heart, and it becomes real to you, you will no longer base your position and your standing in the eyes of God upon how well you have performed. Your reading, praying, church attendance, etc, will no longer be the barometer by which you measure your salvation. All of those things will remain important to you, but for reasons completely unknown before. Miss them, and you will not feel as if you will miss heaven, or as if God is angry, but you will feel hungry, for *He* has become your diet.

Many of us have become drunk on our performance. We are infatuated with external displays of "holiness," and we stand in awe at the Bible study prowess and prayer hours logged by our Christian heroes. To substitute the finished work of Christ on the cross as our confidence and consolation would mean divorcing ourselves from self-worth built upon how much we are doing for Him. This is both difficult and humbling. Difficult, because we have actually emotionally tied ourselves to our performance, feeling good when we perform and bad when we fail; humbling, because to allow the Finished Work to determine our position in Christ is to admit that we are incapable of improving our situation in the least. It's why James 4:6 declares, "God resists the proud, but gives grace to the humble."

The Everlasting Nature of the Blood

No matter how much mixture makes its way into the gospel message, I have yet to meet anyone who advocates a return to animal sacrifice. We are all convinced that Jesus' death on the cross need not be repeated in practice, since He isn't here in the flesh to die anyway. We call His death "once, for all."

Yet the everlasting qualities of His precious blood seem lost on us in our continuing obsession to Judaize the Gospel of Jesus Christ. Animals had to be killed over and over, with new blood applied fresh for every failure, to appease the performance-oriented Old Covenant. That mentality has found its way into our understanding of the blood of Jesus. Due to a temporary consolation, rather than an everlasting one, we present the blood of Jesus as being good until our next sin, and then, just like under an Old Covenant, we have to have it shed all over again.

The author of Hebrews warned his Jewish readers against going back to the system of animal sacrifice by saying that if they fell away from faith in the one sacrifice of Jesus, all of their actions would be paramount to crucifying "again for themselves the Son of God, and put Him to an open shame" (Hebrews 6:6).

This everlasting nature of covenant gives us an everlasting consolation that we are forever beneath the cleansing power of the blood of Jesus. There was a phase of "pleading the blood" over things that swept through the church. People would plead the blood of Jesus over their kids, their wallets, their jobs and their bodies. Most every situation in their lives seemed to be cause for a fresh pleading of the blood. While the intentions were good, the advocates were misinformed. There is no need to plead the blood as if God has forgotten it is there, or to add another layer, as if one layer is not enough! We are FOREVER beneath the blood of Jesus, and this means both in time and in the eternal realm.

Removing the Everlasting Consolation

It seems as if some ministers have an obsession with removing the "everlasting" from our consolation. I say this as one who spent several years under a similar obsession. I felt it was my job to kick people into gear, and to fight against various versions of "lazy Christianity," in which people accepted Christ by faith and then didn't worry about their souls anymore. I mocked sermons on "the love of God," and statements regarding a "gentle Jesus," or the idea that God was anything less than infuriated. To me, someone who believed that he could accept Jesus by faith and then be secure in salvation forever, no matter what they did from that day forward, was either deceived or not really a Christian at all. My definition of everlasting would have included that it was indeed forever, "as long as you lived right."

One tried and true way to remove the everlasting consolation from the believer is to inject works into his grace. If you want to hinder, just tell him what he "needs" to do. By default, the need becomes a command, and a command ignored demands swift retribution. All the "needs" he fails to live up to will carry some sort of punishment, which he can be sure is coming his way. This manipulates people into giving, attending, reading, praying, etc. While our motives are to get them to live "right," our method is flawed with the poisonous addition of works.

> *"And if by grace, then it is no longer of works; otherwise grace is no longer grace. But if it is of works, it is no longer grace; otherwise work is no longer work."* (Romans 11:6)

Grace is no longer grace if works are involved. Work is no longer work when grace does the work. Sounds like a finished work to me!

> *"For by grace you have been saved through faith, and that not of yourselves; it is the gift of God, not of works, lest anyone should boast."* (Ephesians 2:8, 9)

Our salvation came by grace through faith. This grace was not given because God was impressed (and it doesn't remain because God is impressed). Grace is a gift, unearned, for if it were earned in any way, we would boast in every way.

> *"Are you so foolish? Having begun in the Spirit, are you now being made perfect by the flesh?"* (Galatians 3:3)

The Holy Spirit is our beginning. He has been with us since our acceptance of Christ. All things are happening in us and to us because of His presence in our lives. He is completely sufficient to bring about change and modification of all kinds, yet we interfere with our works and effort in some misguided attempt to "help" Him along. How can we expect to be made perfect by the flesh?

Good Hope

Part of what has been given us by the Holy Spirit, in addition to the everlasting consolation, is "good hope." Hope is defined in Greek as a "confident expectation," but it can be of either evil or good. The adjective "good" speaks of the type of hope provided to us by the Holy Spirit.

The everlasting consolation and the good hope are both derived of the same Holy Spirit within us. They cannot be competing, nor can they be separated.

Where there is eternal consolation, there will be good hope, for one who believes he is secure in the capable hands of the Father has good hope founded upon covenant provisions.

Where everlasting consolation breaks down, caused by a mixture of law and grace, good hope is soon to follow. If one has no security in his heart about his position in covenant (and thus, about his salvation), he will find it impossible to hope for good. He may not lose hope entirely, but his optimism will turn to pessimism as he hopes for far less than what the covenant promises, and simply turns to what he thinks he deserves.

The contrast to good hope would be evil hope, which seems both displaced and unnecessary, yet for those of us who have spent many years in the church, we know such a thing exists! Some believers seem more tuned in to bad news than good, almost gravitating toward every scrap of discouraging news. Our end-time eschatology probably has a lot to do with this, as many people are always looking for the last day and they frame their Bible interpretation around events reported on the news and from around the world. Rather than seeing themselves as living in a new era, ripe with Kingdom potential, they spend their time looking for the anti-Christ and trying to identify one-world governments and false prophets.

I did not write this chapter, or this book, to disrupt one's view of world events or Bible prophecy. However, I think every believer should check the adjective in front of their hope. If you are hoping, even subtly, that things go wrong; that the politician you dislike gets caught in corruption; that the best laid plans of men are disrupted and brought to ruin to prove some spiritual point, it is probably time to reevaluate your hope.

To return our hope to the place of its origin – good hope! – we must have a convincing revelation of everlasting consolation. Let these scriptures of consolation and good hope resonate in your heart as we turn the page into the home stretch of our look at the cross of Jesus Christ:

> *"The grace of the Lord Jesus Christ, and the love of God, and the communion of the Holy Spirit be with you all. Amen."* (2 Corinthians 13:14)

"That having been justified by His grace we should become heirs according to the hope of eternal life." (Titus 3:7)

"Blessed be the God and Father of our Lord Jesus Christ, who according to His abundant mercy has begotten us again to a living hope through the resurrection of Jesus Christ from the dead." (1 Peter 1:3)

"I will never leave you nor forsake you." (Hebrews 13:5)

"...lo, I am with you always, even to the end of the age. Amen." (Matthew 28:20)

Chapter 12

His Death Was Your Death

The most fitting way to bring this book to its conclusion is to find our place in the covenant. We have been properly identified as the seed of Abraham due to our faith in Jesus Christ. This entitles us to the blessings of the Abrahamic Covenant. We have seen how the Mosaic Covenant served a role but is now fulfilled, and we are no longer under its performance-based blessings. We rest under the New Covenant, with Christ as our Mediator and High Priest. We function now in a faith-based economy, in which we are blessed based upon Christ's finished work. But the temptation to "help" is bound to creep back into our day-to-day walk. A lifetime of works is not easily shut off. Our old religious tendency to feel as if we should die a little every day can subtly drag us back under the blanket of the Old Covenant.

Stop 'Carrying Your Cross,' 'Dying Daily,' and 'Decreasing'

Most of us are familiar with the very religious idea of "dying daily," or "carrying our cross." These phrases are the buzz words of an idea that has us constantly dying out to our old ways and habits, effectively vanishing, so that the "new you" can shine forth. This concept sounds super-spiritual, but it is blatantly religious, and it is based upon scriptures that have been twisted entirely out of their context.

The New Covenant provisions are NOT dependent upon your death. Your death means nothing in the grand scheme of things, for who could possibly be saved or blessed by your sacrificial offering? In Luke 9:23, Christ told His disciples that if any of them wanted to belong to Him they should deny themselves, take up their cross daily and follow Him. He followed this instruction with a verse that is conveniently left out when attempting to convince people they should be re-crucified. In Luke 9:27, Jesus states that there were some standing there who would not taste death until they saw the Kingdom of God. If Verse 23 means you should die spiritually, why would Jesus change the subject a few verses later with no warning? Since He is speaking of the spreading of the gospel without being ashamed (Verse 26), then He is also speaking of the possibility of physical death to those who minister that gospel. To the disciples, the cross was not a spiritual symbol – like it is to us, on the other side of the crucifixion – but a symbol of execution. To "take up their cross" would not have indicated a daily spiritual death, but the very real possibility that they could die in service of the Master, any day!

A nearly identical passage is found in Paul's writing to the Corinthians, when he declares, "I die daily" (1 Corinthians 15:31). This three-word phrase has been the foundation for entire sermon series! We are encouraged to take up our cross and die a little more every day. While well-intentioned, this is a veiled misunderstanding of what Jesus was accomplishing at Calvary. Paul is in the middle of a treatise on resurrection when he makes his famous statement. His preceding verse asks the perfect question (which gives us our answer): "Why do we stand in jeopardy every hour?" His "die daily" was the same "pick up the cross daily" that Jesus was referring to: the possibility of physical death.

Another passage that is totally misconstrued to establish a sense of daily death is John the Baptist's proclamation, "He must increase, but I must decrease" (John 3:30). This statement should not be spiritualized for believers, for that would indicate there is a low-level of Jesus in us that must grow while the "old man" in us needs to shrink away. This is Old Covenant thinking! John is in the middle of a sermon about the superiority of the one coming after him. He denies that he himself is the Christ, but admits that the Christ is on the way. John saw the necessity in his own ministry vanishing away while Christ's increased in both scope and popularity.

Christ Died for Us

Please forgive the redundancy of this segment title. This entire book has revolved around the theme that Christ died for us. At risk of rehashing the same argument, I must establish the fact one more time with scripture, so that we can build off of that theme our final argument for Calvary.

> *"But God demonstrates His own love toward us, in that while we were still sinners, Christ died for us."* (Romans 5:8)

While Calvary is the ultimate expression of God's love, let's not stop there. He died while we were still lost (in fact, He died 2000 years before we were even born), and did so, "for us." Using the same author (Paul), but a different audience (the church at Galatia), let us add to that thought.

> *"I have been crucified with Christ; it is no longer I who live, but Christ lives in me; and the life which I now live in the flesh I live by faith in the Son of God, who loved me and gave Himself for me."* (Galatians 2:20)

If Romans 5:8 expresses that Christ died for us, then Galatians 2:20 indicates that we were "crucified with Christ." Further into Galatians, in 5:24, Paul declares that those who are Christ's "have crucified the flesh with its passions and desires." Catch the past tense in that passage and see His death on Calvary as a sacrificial one, done on your behalf, and then see your own self crucified there as well. Can you see how the concept of constant crucifixion of self – or "dying daily" – actually cheapens the "once for all" death of Christ?

Now, through another of Paul's epistles, let's put the two ideas together into one verse:

> *"For the love of Christ compels us, because we judge thus: that if One died for all, then all died."* (2 Corinthians 5:14)

In light of all evidence, our final conclusion would be that if the One Man, Christ Jesus, died for all, then His death was the substitutional death of all. Stack all three and you see a progressive revelation of God's Finished Work and His love. The first point is a universally accepted theme of Christianity. The second point takes it further, and is a little harder to swallow for some. The final point is truly the *final point*. Both difficult to grasp and widely rejected, if it becomes real in our hearts, it is the end of all works righteousness:

1. Christ died **for** us.

2. Christ died **as** us.

3. **His** death was **our** death!

The exhaustive feature of the Old Covenant was that no matter how hard a man tried, he could not take away sin. He could not please God through his works and performance. The law declared him guilty and shut his mouth in front of a holy God. Christ's sacrificial death was done on behalf of all law-breakers (both Jew and Gentile) so that we could live instead of die. We do not struggle with the concept of a sacrificial death, but we often wrestle with the idea that He died *as* us, as if He had committed sin. To move on to "His death was our death," is too heady a concept because most of us have not divorced ourselves from the ideas and concepts of the Old Covenant and its performance demands.

To see His death as our death would put finality to the war against sin. It would change our eschatology, framing the scriptures on judgment found in the New Testament within the generation after Jesus, when the temple fell and the Mosaic Economy came tumbling down. His death being our death would mean that *living* was more important than *dying,* and that it is truly acceptable, and even encouraged to "love life and see good days" (1 Peter 3:10).

Appointed for Men to Die Once

I have ministered at countless funerals throughout the years, using a variety of texts and stories depending on the lives of the deceased and the circumstances surrounding their deaths. I'm not alone among ministers in leaning heavily on Hebrews 9:27 as a generic funeral text. It states, "And as it is appointed for men to die once, but after this the judgment." Sounds plain and simple, right?

We proclaim that all men have an appointment with death and then they go on to be judged. This explains why they died and where they are right now. It gives the minister a way out of the age old question "Why did this happen?" as we can answer, "Because it was his time." However, this answer does little in making God look good when the funeral is for a child, whom we can't imagine was appointed to die so young.

Oh what a tangled web we weave when we fail to put scriptures within their contexts! I want to put Hebrews 9:27 in front of you again, but this time I will follow it directly with Verse 28, and you will notice that there is no change of pace or thought, not even a sentence break. Taken as a complete statement, see if anything changes:

> *"And as it is appointed for men to die once, but after this the judgment, so Christ was offered once to bear the sins of many. To those who eagerly wait for Him He will appear a second time, apart from sin, for salvation."* (Hebrews 9:27, 28)

Read together, these two verses do not deny that men will die, but they do confirm that the appointment that all men have "to die once," has been met in the offering of Christ "once." It also states that while post-death brings "the judgment," Jesus was dying "to bear the sins of many." Why does He bear the sins of many with His death? Because man is destined to be judged. Thus, Christ's death was not only sacrificial; it was a death of justice!

The latter half of Verse 28 has little to do with a physical appearing of Jesus, for that would only include those "who eagerly wait for Him." Instead, our eager anticipation of His arrival should be viewed as a revelation of Jesus in our hearts, where He will indeed make an appearance in our life. This appearance will not take place in order to deal with sin (for that has already been dealt with through His birth, death, burial and resurrection). When He appears in your heart, He will deal with your salvation.

Christ dealing with your salvation through a personal, revelatory appearance in your life is completely opposite of the formula used under the Old Covenant. This is a completely different covenant with a superior set of promises. Under performance based religion, you dealt with your own salvation on a daily basis, but under the New Covenant, He works on salvation in you!

Work Out Your Own Salvation

Knowing that he could not be there to assist in their day-to-day walk, Paul encouraged his church at Philippi to "work out your own salvation with fear and trembling," during his absence (Philippians 2:12). This wasn't written as a universal command for all of time, but as a specific one due to his temporary absence from them. To encourage them in this "working out," he reminds them that "it is God who works in you both to will and to do for His good pleasure" (Verse 13). The relevance for us is that whatever we work out of our salvation is due to the fact that God is doing an in-working in our hearts. This statement is not one of grace+works, but rather grace which always leads to works.

The Timing of the Judgment

Hebrews 9:27 says, "after this the judgment," placing man's judgment after his death. Then Verse 28 intervenes and places the death requirement on Jesus "to bear the sins of many." His bearing the sins is to meet the judgment that man is appointed to stand under.

I do not want to remove a future judgment for mankind, but I do want to establish the timing of those judgments on the time clock of heaven. To set dates and times for "end of the world" scenarios has proven to be foolish and uninformed. Whenever and however God chooses to do things is His own prerogative, but we can search the scriptures and find rock solid truths about that judgment. Further, we can also be sure that though our encounter with the judgment may indeed be in the future, in God's eyes, it has already happened.

Jesus was just hours from the cross, having already entered Jerusalem on Palm Sunday. He predicted His own death on the cross, literally calling attention to the method in which He would die. Notice both the timing of the judgment and the manner of death, both in view within two short verses:

> "Now is the judgment of this world; now the ruler of this world will be cast out. And I, if I am lifted up from the earth, will draw all peoples to Myself." (John 12:31, 32)

It sounds like Jesus thought the judgment of the world was about to happen. It was so close that He declared its timing as "Now." Jesus was either right or He was wrong, and I am convinced He knew what He was talking about! The judgment faced by the world happened at the cross of Jesus Christ. Even the ruler of this world's system was cast out when Jesus died on the cross. Not only has the world been judged for its sin and failure, the enemy has been cast from his position of authority and influence. Praise God!

The Ages to Come

References to the "prince of the power of the air" and the "spiritual host of wickedness in the heavenly places," have frightened believers for far too long! Give no confidence or place to the enemy. When Paul spoke of the prince of the power of the air, he stated that he was "according to the course of this world," and that he "now works in the sons of disobedience" (Ephesians 2:2). The course of the world, coupled with the sons of disobedience, speaks of the religious system of Judaism with its courses and familial ties.

The "spiritual host of wickedness in the heavenly places" follows the statement, "against the rulers of the darkness of this age" (Ephesians 6:12). The "age" to which he is referring was the Mosaic Economy and its attached works righteousness. You are not living in that age, for you have passed from death into life; free from a ministry of death, you have a ministry of righteousness. You do not dwell in the darkness of Sinai but rather the light of a heavenly Zion.

In that same letter to the Ephesians, Paul established that believers are seated with Christ "in the heavenly places," indicating not that we have a seat in a place called Heaven, but that we are resting with Him in His finished work. We are seated so that "in the ages to come He might show the exceeding riches of His grace in His kindness toward us in Christ Jesus" (Ephesians 2:7). Paul is looking past the "darkness of this age," in which he was living and writing, and looking forward to the ages to come in which believers would realize their position in Christ. I present to you that we are living in the age for which Paul desired. We are experiencing the riches of God's grace and the kindness of our Lord Jesus like never before, not because we are good, but because we are seated in Him.

"If I be lifted up..."

I don't want to get ahead of myself in this closing chapter, for there is much to cover and all of it is fun! I will get back to the seated Christ in a moment. For now, I want to return to the "Now" statement of Jesus, in which He gave the timing of the world's judgment. The next verse gives the manner of His death:

> "And I, if I am lifted up from the earth, will draw all **peoples** to Myself." (John 12:32)

Notice that I emphasized "peoples." Check your hard copy; it is italicized. If you are using the King James Version it states "men," but it is italicized as well. As stated before, this indicates a word that was added by the translators to complete the thought. Read without that word, it sounds something like, "If I am lifted up from the earth, will draw all to Myself," a statement which demands a previous verse, so that we can ascertain exactly what He is drawing.

That previous verse guarantees the judgment of the world and the ruler being cast out, and says that they are both happening "Now," at the death of Christ. His death was going to be one of a lifting up, which was fulfilled when the Romans lifted Him up on a cross and crucified Him for all to see. This verse is interesting by itself, but it is even more so when you consider that Jesus is simply building on something He has already established.

In His conversation with Nicodemus, Jesus lays out the case for a born again experience. When He comes to the issue of eternal life, He connects His own death to a story involving Moses:

> "And as Moses lifted up the serpent in the wilderness, even so must the Son of Man be lifted up, that whoever believes in Him should not perish but have eternal life." (John 3:14, 15)

This is a direct reference to a story from Israel's past. I say "direct" because Nicodemus would have been very familiar with the Torah, and would have instantly connected Moses' lifting up of the serpent with what Jesus was trying to convey. That story is found in its entirety in Numbers 21:4-9, and because

Jesus used it as a reference for His own death, we can see a crystal clear picture of Christ in its retelling.

The Bronze Serpent

As Israel journeyed from Mount Hor, trekking along the line of the Red Sea around the land of Edom, they spoke out against God and Moses, complaining of the lack of water and showing their displeasure at God's insufficient provision of manna. Seeing as they were functioning beneath the Law of Moses, their murmuring and complaining brought upon them the wrath of God. Poisonous snakes moved among the people and bit many of them, leading to mass death. When the people begged Moses to seek God on their behalf, the Lord gave him instruction:

> "Make a fiery serpent, and set it on a pole; and it shall be that every-
> one who is bitten, when he looks at it, shall live." (Numbers 21:8)

The term "fiery" is a translation for "brazen," which is a type of metal forged by extreme heat. God's instructions were for Moses to fashion a brass snake and attach it to a pole so that it could bring healing to those who gazed upon it. In type, due to the extreme heat involved, brass indicates fiery judgment, like the furnace of God's judgment.

The serpent has long been a type of the enemy, who slithers about in deception. From Eden in Genesis to "that serpent of old" in Revelation 12:9, the snake has indicated both the presence of the enemy and the curse attached to him. Why would God want a brass snake to represent healing for His people?

Jesus claimed that He must be lifted up in the same manner as Moses lifted the serpent in the wilderness. Moses lifted a brass snake, indicating a judged curse, and those who saw it could have life. Jesus suffered the judgment of heaven in our place, and was made to be a curse on our behalf. We have covered these concepts throughout this book, but now we bring them together in one final package. I hope the justice at Calvary is becoming clear!

When Jesus was lifted up above the earth, He did so in the place of judgment. He suffered both the death and the judgment with which mankind had an appointment (Hebrews 9:27). He was made to be a curse so that we could be free from that curse. Anyone who looked upon that snake in the wilderness was healed of the venom in their veins. Anyone who "believes in Him should not perish but have eternal life."

"... I will draw all to Me"

We go back to John 12:32, and our italicized word "peoples." With the subject of judgment being the theme of Verse 31, it's incredible that the translators added the word "peoples," as if the world was the subject. Take a look at Verse 31 again, and ask yourself which is the emphasis: the world or the judgment? The world is being judged at Calvary, and the ruler of the world is being cast out in that judgment. John 16:11 confirms that the ruler of the world has been judged, thus we conclude that Jesus is referring to a complete and total judgment.

He is comparing Himself to the brazen serpent on the pole in the time of Moses. When Moses lifted up the serpent, all venom was drawn out of the veins of the victims. When Jesus was lifted up on the cross, all judgment was drawn into Him, or metaphorically, all death and judgment is drawn out of us when we gaze upon Him by faith.

This makes Hebrews 12:2 so much more appealing, and relevant, when we are "looking unto Jesus, the author and finisher of our faith, who for the joy that was set before Him endured the cross, despising the shame, and has sat down at the right hand of the throne of God." As we look to the brazen serpent on the pole, we are seeing our faith wrapped up in His finished work.

If Jesus draws all judgment into Himself, then you have no fear of a future judgment. Jesus gives us a "most assuredly," which is a rock-solid promise:

> "Most assuredly, I say to you, he who hears My word and believes in Him who sent Me has everlasting life, and shall not come into judgment, but has passed from death into life." (John 5:24)

How can we be sure that we have actually passed from death to life? If our Christianity is not evidenced by the outward show and display of religion, then how can we know who is "saved" and who is "lost?" John wrote another letter in which he addressed that very issue:

> *"We know that we have **passed from death to life**, because we love the brethren. He who does not love his brother abides in death."* (1 John 3:14)

The love of God that resonates in our hearts toward our fellow man is the evidence of the presence of God inside of us. It is our proof that we have no judgment to dread. In fact, John goes a step further to give that blessed assurance to all of his readers:

> *"Love has been perfected among us in this: that we may have **boldness in the day of judgment**; because as He is, so are we in this world."* (1 John 4:17)

The love that was manifested for us at the cross of Christ, in which Christ bore all of the judgment against sin, has now been perfected among us. Due to this perfect love, we can now have boldness in the day of judgment, which in light of these other scriptural facts, indicates that we have no fear of a judgment day. Our lack of fear is not lackadaisical or disrespectful, but rather an acknowledgment that "as He is, so are we in this world."

I find such awesome power in the thought that as Jesus is, so am I, in this present world. Most of us have a religious heritage that encouraged (and browbeat) us to try and be more like Jesus. We were convinced that we were shoddy examples of Christ but that someday "when we all get to Heaven," we would be just like Him. I nearly passed out the day I realized 1 John 4:17 was actually in my Bible!

He is Seated

A few segments ago, we saw Paul's statement of how we are seated together with Christ in heavenly places, and I promised that we would go deeper into the concept of a seated Christ. Now is a fitting moment to do so, as our staring at

Him in Hebrews 12 connects so beautifully with the lifted up Savior of John 12. Also, the passages we just examined in 1 John, Chapters 3 and 4, provide us with guarantees that we have gone from a dead state to a living one because of the love of Christ shown to us at the cross. This gives us boldness in judgment. Watch as Paul connects those thoughts with a seated Savior. I will highlight in bold the phrases that we can connect:

> "But God, who is rich in mercy, because of **His great love with which He loved us**, even when we were **dead in trespasses, made us alive** together with Christ (by grace you have been saved), and raised us up together, and made us **sit together in the heavenly places in Christ Jesus**, that in the ages to come He might show **the exceeding riches of His grace in His kindness toward us** in Christ Jesus." (Ephesians 2:4-7)

The dots are connecting in regards to our salvation in Christ: He loved us immensely, and He proved it by dying in our place, bearing our sins in His body on the tree. We never knew how to live until we were made alive by our acceptance of Christ (saved, by His grace). His resurrection inside of us has declared us as citizens of the heavenly dimension, and in that dimension we are seated with Him in rest. Now, in the ages beyond that of the apostles and of the early church, we are growing daily in the exceeding riches of His grace, and we have continuing revelations of His kindness toward us.

In Chapter 6, we dealt with the superior priesthood of Christ, but there is an interesting fact about His priesthood that we saved for this segment. It ties seamlessly with our being seated with Him, for of what value is it to be seated with Him if we are not convinced of why He is seated?

Under the Old Covenant, the Levitical priesthood was the liaison between man and God. Man was in a constant state of flux and failure so the priesthood was always on the job. Standing between the failures of man and the perfection of God, the priests were a picture of blood and death. They were constantly shedding blood and offering sacrifices and then washing themselves in pure water only to start the endless process all over again.

Due to this merry-go-round of animal sacrifice and physical praise, the Tabernacle of God and the subsequent temples lacked a seemingly essential piece of furniture. No house would be considered complete today without adequate space to rest. Either a chair or a bed would suffice, but we wouldn't call a house a home if there was no comfort to be found inside. However, God's house contained no chairs, couches or beds. This was not an interior design flaw, but a specific withholding designed by God to send a message.

The message is loud and clear when one considers that behind the veil which separated the Holy Place from the Most Holy Place, sat the Ark of the Covenant. On top of that Ark was the Mercy Seat, on which the very presence of God resided. Only God was allowed to take a seat in His house, and even that was behind a veil of judgment. No man could rest there and if one dared enter that room without the blood of a spotless sacrifice, the mercy seat became a judgment seat.

> *"And every priest stands ministering daily and offering repeatedly the same sacrifices, which can never take away sins."* (Hebrews 10:11)

The scripture specifically states that the priest "stands" and repeatedly offers up sacrifices due to the fact that not one of those sacrifices was taking care of the sin issue in the eyes of God.

> *"But this Man, after He had offered one sacrifice for sins forever, sat down at the right hand of God."* (Hebrews 10:12)

The Man is our Lord Jesus Christ. After His death on the cross, which was a one-time sacrifice capable of solving the sin issue, He sat down at God's right hand. The comparison being drawn by the author of Hebrews is that the priests had to stay on their feet when in the service of the tabernacle, for under the law the work is never finished. Conversely, the Great High Priest Jesus offered up one sacrifice and then sat down, since there would never be another sacrifice needed.

The Judgment Seat of Christ

Rather than seeing the Judgment Seat of Christ as a one-time event out in the future somewhere, I see it as an event that every man must encounter at some point. In 2 Corinthians 5:10, Paul said, "For we must all appear before the judgment seat of Christ," and I don't think he was trying to prophesy a date on the calendar. At this seat of judgment, the High Priest is seated for a reason: the work is finished. When Paul concludes the argument, he makes his own judgment call in Verse 14, "that if One died for all, then all died." We used that verse a moment ago to persuade that "His death was our death," but Paul is using it as his final conclusion regarding the judgment seat.

In Romans 14:10, Paul makes a parallel statement when he says, "For we shall all stand before the judgment seat of Christ." Again, Paul has Jesus seated in a place of judgment. Seated, because the work is finished; judgment, because all judgment has been committed into the hands of the Son (John 5:22, 27). Just before this verse Paul makes another conclusion (I hope you are seeing a trend!):

"For to this end Christ died and rose and lived again, that He might be Lord of both the dead and the living." (Romans 14:9)

Again, the judgment seat of Christ is connected with His Finished Work on the cross. His death led to His resurrection, which gave Him the right to be called the Lord of those who are dead and those who are living. By conquering death, He can lord over it since it cannot hold Him. For those who see their death in His death, they can see their new life in His resurrected life. They face the Judgment Seat of Christ with no fear because they know that as He is, so they are!

Where Were You When Jesus Died?

The simple answer to the above question is, "I wasn't even born yet," and of course, you are correct. Keep that in mind the next time you wonder if your future sins were covered by the death of Jesus on the cross! Since you were not yet born, how could you have committed any sin?

I'm not asking in order to find out where we were in the natural realm, but rather where we were in the spiritual. This is not a statement about reincarnation, or some other theory on spirits existing before we were born, but it is a ceremonial one. The question may be better asked, "What if we believe we died when Jesus died?"

This final chapter has been meant to convince you that His death was truly your death, but as I sprint toward the end, I do so with the hope that you actually start to believe it. Paul hoped as much for his Roman readers when he said, "Now if we died with Christ, we believe that we shall also live with Him" (Romans 6:8). I think his use of "if" may have been done to allow the reader to make up his or her own mind. You can believe you died with Him, or not; the choice is yours. If you choose to believe you died with Him, you can further believe that you can also "live with Him."

Paul uses "if" again in regards to our being raised up in Christ, indicating even that takes our faith in order to believe. We may see our death in Him, but do we see our life in Him? Moreover, do we see our life in Christ now or someday in a futuristic Heaven?

> *"If then you were raised with Christ, seek those things which are above, where Christ is, sitting at the right hand of God. Set your mind on things above, not on things on the earth."* (Colossians 3:1, 2)

Once again we find Christ sitting at the Father's right hand – the place of power and authority. Having been raised in a newness of life through Christ's resurrection, we now set our minds on a higher realm. We are not earth-bound in our hope or our assurance, due to the fact that we have been raised up into the life of the heavenly One.

> *"For you died, and your life is hidden with Christ in God."* (Colossians 3:3)

At the cross of Jesus Christ, you died. The life which you now live in the flesh, you live by the faith of the Son of God, who is passionately in love with you (Galatians 2:20). Everything about you that appears on the surface, and that is tucked away in your heart, is now hidden. Christ enwraps you like a cocoon, covering over your failures, fears and insecurities. When God looks at you, He sees only His Son, covering you over with great wings of love, like a hen gathers in her chicks. The precious and everlasting blood of a New Covenant has been smeared like rainproof paint over the door of your heart, and due to its lasting nature, the angel of death is forced to pass over you. His blood indicates that a death has occurred already, and that only the living remains here.

"When Christ who is our life appears, then you also will appear with Him in glory." (Colossians 3:4)

Within context, I don't think Paul is referring to a physical appearing of Christ in your future as much as he is referencing Christ appearing in our New Creation existence. He is our life now, not merely in the timeless future. When He appears in the believer, we begin to appear with Him in all of His glory. This is how John could justify telling us that "as He is, so are we in this world," and also, "it has not yet been revealed what we shall be, but we know that when He is revealed, we shall be like Him, for we shall see Him as He is" (1 John 4:17 & 1 John 3:2). Just as Paul said in 2 Corinthians 3:18, as we behold, "as in a mirror the glory of the Lord, we are being transformed into the same image from glory to glory, just as by the Spirit of the Lord."

Patience, My Friend

You may see very little of the precious qualities of our lovely Jesus shining through in your life at this point. It is a revelatory step to go from a Christianity based upon the mixture of law and grace and into one of resting in the Finished Work of Jesus. Our cultural conviction may even scream out that we are making a false step into deception when we finally shake free of the chains of religion and obligation. As we humbly go forth into our rightful inheritance as sons instead of into another day of labor as slaves, our system, which has been so finely tuned toward our own works, may sense that the New Covenant is a foreign invader, and it may work hard to expel it. The process is slow and patience is required, for the work of the Spirit is pure and tender.

"For ye have need of patience, that, after ye have done the will of God, ye might receive the promise." (Hebrews 10:36, KJV)

The heartbeat of this entire book has been the covenants that God has operated under and the promises attached to those covenants. As we have identified what covenant we are functioning beneath, we have been able to shed light on the glorious promises of this New Covenant. The receiving of promises is the believer's highest honor. We receive as a free gift, what cost God everything. He has "given to us exceedingly great and precious promises," which makes us "partakers of the divine nature" (2 Peter 2:4).

Notice that as we receive these great and precious promises we become partakers of the divine nature. Believers that have little to no covenant knowledge will also partake very little in the nature of the divine. Also, if we feel that we can "earn our grace" or pay God back through our efforts then we are handcuffed from receiving His promises as a gift. Once the promises go back underneath the condition of works, the new garment is patched with an old cloth and we partake of our own efforts instead of His nature. The key that unlocks the glorious wonders of this New Covenant is to simply be a receiver.

"After You Have Done the Will of God"

One final glimpse at context is necessary in order to put a lid on the topic for now. I say "for now," because I realize that we haven't come close to exhausting the subject of covenant. In fact, I'm not sure we have really even started. Revelation of who Jesus is and who we are in Him is ongoing, and I for one am excited to know that there is more to learn.

When the writer of Hebrews tells his audience to be patient after they have done the will of God, he is referring back to a portion from the same chapter. In Hebrews 10:9 we see that Jesus had come "To do Your will, O God," and that He "takes away the first that He may establish the second." We have already learned that He was taking away the first covenant to establish the second. Then the author pegs exactly what was God's will:

> "By that will we have been sanctified through the offering of the body of Jesus Christ once for all." (Hebrews 10:10)

God's will was that Jesus be the offering for sin, "once for all." He was tired of the inefficient and insufficient sacrificial system of the Mosaic Covenant. He had instituted it, but not for righteousness. Now, to make men righteous, it was God's will that it all be finished in one fell swoop. His will having been done, we have been sanctified (set aside) as God's new chosen people. No longer confined to a piece of real estate on the map, His nation and His people are part and parcel with His will. Once we have placed our faith in what was His perfect will, all we need now is patience, so that we "may receive the promise."

Now Have Obtained Mercy

The New Covenant changed everything. It brought man back into right fellowship with God, reconciling us to Him through the sacrificial offering of His perfect Son. It is everlasting and full of the life of the everlasting realm. It provides promises and hope and an eternal consolation to all who rest beneath its umbrella. It is better, with better promises. It is established on finished work rather than unfinished work. It declares us just, forgiven and favored.

The cross was the sign, seal and symbol of God's Covenant. What happened there will stand for both time and eternity, for both are wrapped up in it. Man's accessibility to God goes through the cross beams of Calvary, where the ground is indeed level and there is liberty and justice for all. Though the provisions of our covenant may have been birthed in Abraham, they were guaranteed in Christ, and there is no more solid guarantee to be found.

Like nothing before, the New Covenant gives unidentifiable man the identity of God: chosen by Him, royal like Him, holy like Him and special in His eyes. The Apostle Peter sums it up perfectly, and we will use his statement as our closing one.

> "But you are a chosen generation, a royal priesthood, a holy nation, His own special people, that you may proclaim the praises of Him who called you out of darkness into His marvelous light; who once were not a people but are now the people of God, who had not obtained mercy but now have obtained mercy." (1 Peter 2:9-10)

Epilogue

Each author has his or her own unique style. Personally, I would rather preach than write, but the medium of writing has such lasting impact, allowing the reader to move at his own pace, that it is necessary to write things down from time to time. I do this with great reluctance due to the nature of the material and the fact that revelation is a progression. What I know today should be a building block for what I will learn tomorrow. Thus, today's writing may feel incomplete in just a short time. My style is to work things out as I go, sometimes circling back onto the theme again and again while trying to build a case through different streams of thought. My prayer is that it has been both easy and fun to follow along.

I go into writing a book much like I would a sermon, with a thought and a few ideas toward getting that thought across. In the midst of a sermon, spontaneity takes over and things come and go that no preparation has been made for. I call these moments, "chasing rabbits;" a hunting/hiking term meant to indicate that a bunny has crossed the trail and the dogs are now both off the trail and on its scent. While I'm working my way toward an intended goal, I get distracted at chasing down these "minor" thoughts, which often become major ones.

While I have one major thought, which the title encapsulates, the chapters are supporting themes. Within them, the "rabbits" often hop and ground is covered, even if it was not the ground I set out to traverse. All in all, we arrive where we set out to go and hopefully the composite whole is more than a spider-web of themes and ideas. In this particular case, I hope we have arrived right back where we started, as eye-witnesses near the foot of the cross.

The scriptures that make up the foundation of my sermons and my writings are often pre-determined as support for the idea. Sometimes, however, they come through research and cross-reference. Better yet are the scriptures that pop up unexpectedly, a product of a lifetime of reading and memorizing. These are often verses I have used in other settings, or felt had alternate meanings. They float into my spirit and settle onto the page in what may appear to be random order. Time and experience has taught me that there is usually nothing random about it.

I have a slight obsession with first and last. I love stories of the first person to accomplish something as well as the last words of famous people. I have built sermons out of biblical first mentions, and how they affected the scripture narrative from there on. I have also preached the famous last words of the apostles as found in their epistles. You are probably not shocked to learn that the last recorded words of Peter, John and Paul all included the word, "grace."

It is the lack of randomness and my infatuation with the first and the last that brought me to the final conclusion of this book. In Chapter 1, the first scripture I quoted even partially was from 1 Peter. In my final chapter (12), the final scripture quotation is from 1 Peter as well. This was not done intentionally, but due to the book squeezed in between these two passages, I am again convinced there was nothing random about it.

To keep you from having to peruse the book to find them, here they are:

"He indeed was foreordained before the foundation of the world, but was manifest in these last times for you." (1 Peter 1:20)

"But you are a chosen generation, a royal priesthood, a holy nation, His own special people, that you may proclaim the praises of Him who called you out of darkness into His marvelous light; who once were not a people but are now the people of God, who had not obtained mercy but now have obtained mercy." (2 Peter 2:9, 10)

Back-to-back we see the underlying story of this book. Christ was ordained to come in the human form of Jesus, for all of mankind. Because He came, we are the chosen generation, the royal priesthood, the holy nation, etc. What we lost in the beginning we get back in this present hour. Because of His manifestation, we have obtained mercy.

The previous paragraph is what I hope to have accomplished through the writing of this book. The bookend scriptures, with lots of themes and rabbit-trails in between, are meant to establish covenantal knowledge and an eternal consolation.

I haven't intentionally run into controversial themes or topics, though I'm sure a bit of controversy will follow. Some of the things covered are in such detail as to leave little wonder as to where I stand, while others are ambiguous enough to leave the reader curious. This is intentional, for on many of these topics, even the author is still trying to figure it out.

The end-all book on the covenants has yet to be written – not even the Bible itself claimed to cover every area of the riches of God's grace. Some of these glorious riches are mined by prospecting believers in search of the things of God. Graduation past feeling that we must search **for God** is necessary. Only when we arrive at such a state – which the Finished Work has paid for – do we begin to search for the truths **about God.**

Perhaps we have helped. If so, I am most humbled. May your journey into the truths of the New Covenant continue and never grow old. As Peter wrote, "Grace and peace by multiplied to you in the knowledge of God and of Jesus our Lord" (2 Peter 1:2).